NATIONAL 1ST EDITION

BANKRUPTCY

IS IT THE RIGHT
SOLUTION TO YOUR
DEBT PROBLEMS?

by **Attorney Robin Leonard**

Edited by Stephen Elias

nolo

Keeping Up to Date

To keep its books up-to-date, Nolo issues new printings and new editions periodically. New printings reflect minor legal changes and technical corrections. New editions contain major legal changes, major text additions or major reorganizations. To find out if a later printing or edition of any Nolo book is available, call Nolo at 510-549-1976 or check our website at www.nolo.com.

To stay current, follow the "Update" service at our website at www.nolo.com. In another effort to help you use Nolo's latest materials, we offer a 35% discount off the purchase of the new edition of your Nolo book when you turn in the cover of an earlier edition. (See the "Special Upgrade Offer" in the back of the book.)

This book was last revised in: **MAY 2000.**

FIRST EDITION

Second Printing	May 2000
Editor	Stephen Elias
Illustrations	Mari Stein
Cover Design	Toni Ihara
Index	Sayre Van Young
Production	Amy Ihara
Proofreading	Joe Sadusky
Printing	Versa Press Inc.

Leonard, Robin.
    Bankruptcy : is it the right solution to your debt problems? / by Robin Leonard.
      p. cm.
    Includes index.
    ISBN 0-87337-449-5
    1. Bankruptcy—United States—Popular works. 2. Finance, Personal—United States. I. Title.
    HG3766.L37 1998
    332.7'5'0973—dc21

98-27090
CIP

Quantity sales: For information on bulk purchases or corporate premium sales, please contact the Special Sales department. For academic sales or textbook adoptions, ask for Academic Sales. 800-955-4775, Nolo.com, 950 Parker St., Berkeley, CA, 94710.

Acknowledgments

Thanks, Steve. It's always a pleasure and a challenge to work with you.

Table of Contents

1. What Is Bankruptcy?

2. Who Can File for Bankruptcy?

3. Will I Wipe Out My Debts?

4. Will I Lose My House or Apartment?

5. Can I Keep My Car and Other Vital Items of Property?

6. Can I Keep My Credit Cards?

7. Will I Lose My Job, Children, Freedom or Self-Respect?

8. Is It Too Hard to File?

9. Will I Be Able to Get Credit in the Future?

10. Can Some Alternative Outside of Bankruptcy Do the Trick?

11. What If the Bankruptcy Law Changes?

Checklist

Index

What Is Bankruptcy?

Jonathan and Hilda are married with two young children. Hilda is a stay-at-home mother. They had always managed their money wisely until disaster struck: the large corporation for which Jonathan was working merged with its competitor and Jonathan was downsized out of a job. He was out of work for several months, during which time he and Hilda relied heavily on their credit cards. He found a job with a small start-up company for less pay and with fewer benefits than his prior job. Jonathan and Hilda tried hard to catch up on their bills, but couldn't and, in fact, got much further behind. After a year of working for the new job, Jonathan was out of work again when the company went belly up. He found work again fairly quickly, but during the six weeks he was unemployed he and Hilda again charged necessities on their credit cards. With interest charges mounting, Jonathan and Hilda now owe over $30,000 on five credit cards.

Long-time friends David and Charlotte first dreamed of opening a business together when they met in their graphic arts class in college. Two years ago, their dream came true when they started Dalotte Designs. They borrowed money from friends and relatives and took cash advances on their credit cards to purchase the equipment and inventory they needed to get started. Business was good for a while, but their dream turned into a nightmare when their primary client, the local university, decided to do all its design work in-house. Although David and Charlotte found new clients, none provided them with enough work to keep their business going. While Charlotte's relatives forgave her the debts she owed them and even gave her money to pay off her other debts, David wasn't so lucky. He owes friends, relatives, credit card companies and half of the business' creditors over $25,000.

When Carly divorced, she agreed to take less than 50% of the marital property in exchange for her husband, Miles, agreeing to pay most of the marital debts. Miles has since defaulted on the accounts, and the creditors are pursuing her. Carly has kept them away for several months, but a few are threatening to sue her and garnish her wages. Her credit is damaged, and the account balances keep rising because of finance charges and late fees. In total, the creditors and collection agencies claim she owes $17,000 because of Miles' defaults.

Larry owes doctors and hospitals $82,000 for the unsuccessful experimental treatment his now-deceased wife received while battling a rare illness. Neither Larry's nor his wife's health insurance would cover the procedure. Larry has tried mightily to negotiate the amount down to something he can afford, but the collection agencies now trying to collect the debts won't budge. In fact, they are making life miserable for Larry and his eight-year-old daughter.

Even if your situation isn't identical to Jonathan and Hilda's, David's, Carly's or Larry's, you probably can see some similarities between their stories and your own. You have more debt than you can handle. Your debt mushroomed because of circumstances beyond your control—job loss, divorce, business failure, illness, accident, death or unreasonable creditors unwilling to help you out. You feel overwhelmed and are considering your options. Maybe a friend, relative or even a lawyer suggested bankruptcy, describing it as the best thing in the world for you. Someone else may have said the opposite—that bankruptcy is a huge mistake and will ruin your life. Right now, you're filled with emotional turmoil—confusion, fear, guilt, anguish. You don't know what bankruptcy is, whether or not it can help you or what it would mean for your future.

Relax. You're not alone. Since 1996, well over one million Americans file for bankruptcy each year. So do hundreds of companies. Some of the most heated debates in Congress focus on our bankruptcy laws. Bankruptcy has become a necessary and pervasive part of our economic system.

And bankruptcy may be right for you. For a fee of $185-$200 and the cost of a self-help law book, you may be able to wipe out all or most of your debts, or get help from the bankruptcy court while you repay some or all of your debts. If you're deep in debt, bankruptcy may seem like a magic wand. It often is.

But bankruptcy has its drawbacks, too. Before you decide to file, you need to understand the different types of bankruptcies, what bankruptcy can and cannot do for you and the long-term effect of bankruptcy.

There is no formula to use to figure out if bankruptcy is right for you. Nevertheless, anyone considering filing for bankruptcy must spend some time examining their property, the amount of their debts, the types of their debts, their income, their recent financial transactions and the intensity of the efforts their creditors are making to collect what they are due.

Keep in mind that bankruptcy may not be your only option. Chapter 10 explores some of the other options and includes references to books that can help you handle your debts outside of bankruptcy.

A. Types of Bankruptcies

Congress has devised two kinds of bankruptcy: liquidation and reorganization. In a liquidation bankruptcy, your nonessential property items may be sold to pay down your debt. The liquidation bankruptcy is called Chapter 7 bankruptcy, and can be filed by individuals (a "consumer Chapter 7 bankruptcy") or businesses (a "business Chapter 7 bankruptcy"). A Chapter 7 bankruptcy typically lasts three to six months.

In a reorganization bankruptcy, you devote part of your income to pay down your debt. There are three different kinds of reorganization bankruptcies:

- Chapter 13 bankruptcies for individuals (usually lasts three to five years)
- Chapter 11 bankruptcies for individuals with very high debts and for businesses (may last a few months or several years), and
- Chapter 12 bankruptcies for individuals for whom the bulk of their debts come from the operation of a family farm (usually lasts three to five years).

This book discusses only consumer Chapter 7 bankruptcies and Chapter 13 bankruptcies.

While lawyers and judges may refer to bankruptcies as "liquidation" and "reorganization," you don't have to. To distinguish between a consumer Chapter 7 bankruptcy and a Chapter 13 bankruptcy, use language that make sense to you—such as a bankruptcy where my property is used to pay my debts versus a bankruptcy where my income is used to pay my debts, or the bankruptcy that takes a few months versus the bankruptcy that takes a few years.

1. Chapter 7 Bankruptcy

In a Chapter 7 bankruptcy, you are provided the opportunity to cancel, or discharge, certain types of debts in exchange for giving up certain types of property to be sold for the benefit of your creditors. As distressing as this may sound, most debtors are able to hang on to property they need to get on with their lives, and in fact most debtors keep all of their property.

 Chapters 4 and 5 explain what property you are at risk of losing in a bankruptcy case.

The Chapter 7 bankruptcy process takes about four to six months, currently costs $200 in filing and administrative fees and commonly requires one trip to the courthouse. To begin a Chapter 7 bankruptcy case, you fill out several forms (shown in Chapter 8, Section A) and file them with the bankruptcy court in your area. The forms ask you to describe:

- your property
- your current income and its sources
- your current monthly living expenses
- your debts
- property you are allowed to keep through bankruptcy (called exempt property)
- property owned and money spent during the previous two years, and
- property sold or given away during the previous two years.

 Chapter 7 bankruptcy has a few eligibility requirements. These are explained in Chapter 2.

In most Chapter 7 bankruptcies, the majority—if not all—of your debts are discharged by the court at the end of the case. This means that you will no longer owe money to those creditors. In some bankruptcies, certain debts survive the bankruptcy intact, meaning you will still owe those creditors the money you owed when you filed your bankruptcy papers, plus the interest that stopped accruing during your case.

In rare situations, a judge may ask you to come to court at the end of your case. More likely, however, you will be sent a court paper stating that your case is over. Unfortunately, that paper doesn't specify which of your debts were discharged and which were not. It simply states that all debts that qualified for discharge have been discharged.

If you file for bankruptcy and then change your mind, you can ask the court to dismiss your case. As a general rule, a court will dismiss a Chapter 7 bankruptcy as long as the dismissal won't harm your creditors. Usually, you can file again if you want to, although you may have to wait 180 days and you will have to pay a new filing fee.

2. Chapter 13 Bankruptcy

Chapter 13 bankruptcy, sometimes called the wage earner's plan, is quite different from Chapter 7 bankruptcy. In a Chapter 13 bankruptcy, you use your income to pay some or all of what you owe to your creditors. Most Chapter 13 bankruptcies last three years. Some last longer—a court can approve a case as long as five years. A few are shorter—if you pay off 100% of your debts in less than three years, your case will be over sooner. Chapter 13 bankruptcy isn't for everyone. If your total debt burden is too high or your income is too low or irregular, you may not be eligible.

To file for Chapter 13 bankruptcy, you must have a steady income. Furthermore, your secured debts cannot exceed $807,750 and your unsecured debts cannot be more than $269,250. A secured debt is one that gives a creditor the right to take a specific item of property (such as your house or car) if you don't pay it; an unsecured debt doesn't give the creditor this right—common examples of unsecured debts are credit cards and medical bills. Currently, it costs $185 to file for Chapter 13 bankruptcy.

To begin a Chapter 13 bankruptcy, you fill out a packet of forms—much like the forms in a Chapter 7 bankruptcy—listing your income, property, expenses and debts, and file them with a nearby bankruptcy court. In addition, you must file a workable plan, given your income and expenses. Under the plan, you make payments, usually monthly, to the bankruptcy trustee, an official appointed by the bankruptcy court to oversee your case. (Section C, below, discusses the trustee.) The trustee in turn pays your creditors.

In a Chapter 13 bankruptcy, some creditors are entitled to receive 100% of what you owe while others may receive a much smaller percentage. Typically, creditors in a Chapter 13 bankruptcy are paid as follows:

- **Administrative claims** are paid 100%—these include fees owed to the bankruptcy court, including your filing fee, and attorney's fees, if you hire an attorney for help with your Chapter 13 bankruptcy.
- **Priority debts** are paid 100%—these include up to $4,300 in wages, salaries or commissions you owe anyone who worked for you within 90 days before you filed for bankruptcy, contributions you owe to an employee benefit fund, alimony and child support and certain tax debts.
- **Mortgage defaults** are paid 100% if you want to keep your house.
- **Other secured debt defaults**, such as missed car payments, are usually paid 100% if you want to keep the property. It may be possible to pay less.
- **Unsecured debts** are paid anywhere from 0% to 100% of what you owe. The exact amount depends on the value of your nonexempt property, the amount of disposable income you have each month to put toward your debts, how long your plan lasts and the attitude of your local bankruptcy court. Some courts have no problem approving a Chapter 13 plan that proposes to repay very little or nothing to unsecured creditors. Other courts refuse to approve a plan that proposes paying anything less than 70%.

If your bankruptcy lasts a full three- or five-year period, the remaining unpaid balance on your debts that qualify for discharge will be wiped out at the end of your case. If any balance remains on a debt that doesn't qualify for discharge, you will continue to owe it. (The debts that qualify for discharge are explained in Chapter 3.)

If, for some reason, you cannot make some payments under your Chapter 13 plan, you can ask the bankruptcy court to modify it. As long as it's clear that you're acting in good faith, the court is likely to approve a request for a modification. If you won't be able to complete the plan because of circumstances beyond your control, the court might let you discharge the remainder of your debts on the basis of hardship.

If the bankruptcy court won't let you modify your plan or give you a hardship discharge, you can:

- convert your Chapter 13 bankruptcy to a Chapter 7 bankruptcy, unless you received a Chapter 7 discharge within the previous six years (this is explained in Chapter 2), or
- dismiss your Chapter 13 case, which means you'll owe your creditors the balances on your debts from before you filed your Chapter 13 case, less the payments you made, plus the interest that stopped accruing while your Chapter 13 case was open.

As you may have concluded, Chapter 13 bankruptcy requires discipline. For the entire length of your case, you will have to live under a strict budget; the bankruptcy court will not allow you to spend money on anything it deems nonessential. The majority of debtors never complete their Chapter 13 plans—only about 35% do. Many drop out very early in the process, without ever submitting a feasible repayment plan to the court. Nevertheless, for the 35% of those who do make it, the rewards can be high.

3. Reasons to Choose One Type of Bankruptcy Over the Other

In most parts of the country, the majority of people who file for bankruptcy file a Chapter 7 case. For example, during one 12-month period, 957,117 individuals filed for Chapter 7 bankruptcy, while 391,930 people filed for Chapter 13.

In a few places, however, Chapter 13 filings far exceed, equal or near the Chapter 7 filings. This is true in parts of Alabama, Arkansas, Georgia, Louisiana, Mississippi, North Carolina, South Carolina, Tennessee, Texas and Utah.

Neither of these trends is surprising. Most people choose Chapter 7 bankruptcy because it is fast, effective and easy to file. In the majority of situations, a case is opened and closed within six months and the person filing emerges debt-free. (Some people who file for Chapter 7 bankruptcy still owe money on certain debts when their case is over. These nondischargeable debts are described in Chapter 3.)

In addition, few individuals lose any property in Chapter 7 bankruptcy. (Some people who file for Chapter 7 bankruptcy do lose property, however. The categories of nonexempt property are explained in Chapters 4 and 5.)

Finally, many individuals in the south and in Utah—recognized as highly religious parts of the country—have a moral objection to not paying their debts. In those places, Chapter 13 filings are much higher than average.

Moral issues aside, there are many reasons why people who qualify for both to choose Chapter 13 bankruptcy instead of Chapter 7 bankruptcy. (Eligibility is covered in Chapter 2.) Generally, you are probably a good candidate for Chapter 13 bankruptcy if you are in any of the following situations:

- You are behind on your mortgage or car loan, and want to make up the missed payments over time and reinstate the original agreement. You generally cannot do this in Chapter 7 bankruptcy.
- You have a tax obligation, student loan or other debt that cannot be discharged in Chapter 7 bankruptcy, but can be paid off over time in a Chapter 13 plan. (Nondischargeable debts are discussed in Chapter 3.)
- You have a sincere desire to repay your debts, but you need the protection of the bankruptcy court to do so.

B. Filing for Bankruptcy Stops Your Creditors

When you file for any kind of bankruptcy, something called the "automatic stay" goes into effect. The automatic stay prohibits virtually all creditors from taking any action directed at collecting the debts you owe them unless the bankruptcy court says otherwise. In general, creditors cannot:

- take any collection activities, such as sending you letters or calling you
- file a lawsuit or proceed with a pending lawsuit against you
- terminate utilities or public benefits, such as welfare or food stamps
- record liens against your property, or

- seize your property, such as the money in a bank account.

If a creditor tries to collect a debt in violation of the automatic stay, you can ask the bankruptcy court to hold the creditor in contempt of court and to fine the creditor.

There are some notable exceptions to the automatic stay. The following proceedings can continue:

- A criminal proceeding. If it can be broken down into criminal and debt components, the criminal component will be allowed to continue. For example, if you were convicted of writing a bad check and have been sentenced to community service and ordered to pay a fine, your obligation to do community service will not be stopped by the automatic stay.

- A lawsuit that seeks to establish your paternity of a child or to establish, modify or collect child support or alimony.

- A tax audit, the issuance of a tax deficiency notice, a demand for a tax return, the issuance of a tax assessment and the demand for payment of such an assessment by the IRS. The automatic stay, however, does stop the IRS from issuing a lien or seizing any of your property.

The automatic stay may be lifted by the bankruptcy court as it applies to a particular creditor if that creditor convinces the court that the stay isn't serving its intended purpose: to freeze your assets and debts so that the court can deal with them. The stay can be lifted within a week or two, though a few months is more common. Here is how the automatic stay affects some common emergencies:

- **Utility disconnection.** If you're behind on a utility bill and the company is threatening to disconnect your water, electric, gas or telephone service, the automatic stay will prevent the disconnection for at least 20 days. Bankruptcy will probably discharge the past due debts for utility service, although the amount of a utility bill itself rarely justifies a bankruptcy filing.

- **Foreclosure.** If your home mortgage is being foreclosed on, the automatic stay temporarily stops the proceedings, but the creditor will often be able to proceed with the foreclosure sooner or later. (See Chapter 4 for more information.)

- **Eviction.** If you are being evicted from your home, the automatic stay can usually buy you a few days or a few weeks. But if the landlord asks the court to lift the stay and let the eviction proceed— which landlords usually do—the court will probably agree, reasoning that eviction won't affect the bankruptcy. Despite the attractiveness of even a temporary delay, it is seldom a good idea to file for bankruptcy solely because you're being evicted.

- **Enforcement of child support or alimony.** If you owe child support or alimony, bankruptcy will not interrupt your obligation to make current payments. And, as mentioned above, the automatic stay does not stop proceedings to establish, modify or collect back support.

- **Loss of driver's license because of liability for damages.** In some states, your driver's license may be suspended until you pay a court judgment for damages resulting from an automobile accident. The automatic stay can prevent this suspension if it hasn't already occurred. If you are absolutely dependent on your ability to drive for your livelihood and family support, keeping your driver's license can be a powerful reason to file for bankruptcy.

C. Bankruptcy Trustee

Until your Chapter 7 or Chapter 13 bankruptcy case ends, your financial problems are in the hands of the bankruptcy court. With little exception, the court assumes legal control of your property and debts as of the date you file. If you sell or give away property or pay off any debts while your case open without the court's consent, you risk having your case dismissed. The court exercises its control through a court-appointed person called a bankruptcy trustee. The trustee's primary duty is to see that your unsecured creditors are paid as much as possible on the debts you owe them.

The trustee may be a local bankruptcy attorney, very knowledgeable about Chapter 7 or Chapter 13 bankruptcy generally and the local court's rules and procedures specifically. In some courts, trustees are not attorneys, but are business people with specialized knowledge of finances or personal bankruptcy.

Just a few days after you file your bankruptcy papers, you'll get a Notice of Appointment of Trustee from the court, giving the name, address and phone number of the trustee. The letter may also include a list of any financial documents the trustee wants copies of, such as bank statements, canceled checks and tax returns, and the date by which the trustee wants them. (These documents are usually required in Chapter 13 cases only.)

1. Chapter 7 Trustee

In a Chapter 7 bankruptcy, the trustee is mostly interested in what you own and what property you claim as exempt. The more assets the trustee recovers for your creditors, the more the trustee is paid.

Shortly after you file for bankruptcy, the trustee reads the forms you filed. The trustee decides, based on your papers, whether you have enough nonexempt property to sell to raise cash to pay your creditors. If you don't—and most people don't—your bankruptcy is called a no-asset case. If you do, your bankruptcy is called an asset case.

The trustee then sends a notice of your bankruptcy filing to all the creditors you listed. The notice tells the creditors whether or not they should file claims—that is, request to be paid. In no-asset cases, the trustee will tell them not to bother.

A short time later, the trustee asks you questions based on the papers you filed at a short hearing called the creditors' meeting (discussed in Section D.1.a, below). After this meeting, the trustee will begin paying your creditors, if you have any nonexempt property. You will be asked to surrender the property to the trustee, pay the trustee its fair market value or, if the trustee agrees, swap some exempt property of equal value for the nonexempt property. If the nonexempt property isn't worth very much or would be cumbersome for the trustee to sell, the trustee can abandon the property—which means you get to keep it.

2. Chapter 13 Trustee

In a Chapter 13 bankruptcy, the trustee's primary role is to receive your payments and distribute them pro rata to your creditors. The trustee is paid by keeping a percentage of the payments you make—anywhere from 3% to 10%.

Many Chapter 13 trustees play a fairly active role in the cases they administer. This is especially true in small suburban or rural judicial districts or districts with a lot of Chapter 13 bankruptcy cases. For example, a trustee may:

- give you financial advice and assistance, such as helping you create a realistic budget (the trustee cannot, however, give you legal advice)
- actively participate in helping you modify your plan, if necessary
- give you a temporary reprieve or take other steps to help you get back on track if you miss a payment or two, or
- participate at any hearing on the value of an item of property, possibly even hiring an appraiser.

Despite the trustee's great interest in your finances, your financial relationship with the trustee is not as stifling as it may sound. In most situations, you keep complete control over money and property you acquire after filing—as long as you make the payments called for under your repayment plan, and you make all regular payments on your secured debts.

D. Going to Court

In all bankruptcy cases, you will have to make at least one court appearance, and sometimes two.

1. Chapter 7 Bankruptcy

In most Chapter 7 bankruptcy cases, you will make only one court appearance. But bankruptcy is an informal administrative process. It is not a formal adversarial lawsuit, although it can become that in rare cases. Your court appearance will probably remind you of sitting around a conference table at work. Don't think *Law and Order* or *The Practice.*

a. Meeting of the Creditors

As mentioned just above, after you file for bankruptcy, the trustee will send notice to your creditors—and to you—of a hearing called the meeting of creditors. This meeting is usually 20-40 days after you file. Most bankruptcy courts set aside one or two days a month to hold Chapter 7 bankruptcy creditors' meetings. When you show up for your meeting, many other people who have filed for bankruptcy will be there, too. And more than likely, everyone was told to come at the same time. Fifty or more cases may all be scheduled for 9:00 a.m. Bring a book to read or plan on spending time watching a bunch of other cases before your turn is called.

Almost always, the creditors' meeting is brief—usually less than five minutes. You must attend. Despite the meeting's name, creditors rarely do. The trustee asks you some questions about information in your forms. The trustee is likely to be most interested in:

- anticipated tax refunds
- any possible right that you have to sue someone because of a recent accident or business loss
- recent large payments to creditors or relatives, and
- finding out if you paid someone other than a lawyer, such as a bankruptcy petition preparer (see Chapter 8, Section B), to help you file your papers.

In rare situations, if your papers give any indication that you own valuable nonexempt property, the trustee may question you vigorously. You may also be questioned about why you claimed certain property as exempt.

When the trustee is finished, any creditors who showed up are given a chance to question you. They may seek clarification of anything unclear on your forms or propose terms of an agreement for you to agree to pay a debt after your bankruptcy case ends. (This is called reaffirming a debt.)

A creditor might also ask for an explanation if information in your bankruptcy papers differs from what was on your credit application. If you lied about your income, debts or something else important on a credit application, the creditor may claim that you committed fraud and therefore should not be allowed to discharge that creditor's debt.

When the trustee and creditors are through asking questions, you're dismissed.

b. Relief From Stay Hearing

A relief from stay hearing may be requested by a creditor who wants to pursue collection efforts against you. This could come up, for example, if you are behind on your mortgage payments. Because you cannot fix your default and get back on track with payments in a Chapter 7 bankruptcy, the creditor may ask the court to let it begin or continue any foreclosure proceedings.

c. Discharge Hearing

Years ago, before bankruptcy filings increased so dramatically, debtors were required to attend a discharge hearing at the end of their case. Today, a court will require you to come to a discharge hearing only if you agree to reaffirm a debt. At the hearing, the judge will warn you of the consequences of reaffirmation: you'll continue to owe the full debt, you may lose the collateral and the creditor can sue you if you default on your payments. (Reaffirmation is discussed in Chapter 5, Section C.4.)

2. Chapter 13 Bankruptcy

A Chapter 13 bankruptcy case requires at least two court appearances, and sometimes as many as four or five. These court appearances aren't anything like full-blown trials; they're usually brief hearings where you appear before the trustee or judge for just a few minutes.

a. Meeting of the Creditors

The meeting of the creditors is the first court appearance you must make. It's fairly routine and usually something you can handle easily without an attorney. As with Chapter 7 bankruptcies, most bankruptcy courts set aside one or two days a month to hold Chapter 13 bankruptcy creditors' meetings. This means that when you show up for your meeting, many other people who are in a similar situation will be there, too, having been told to come the same time you were told to be there. You may have to wait several hours before your case is called.

Your creditors' meeting, if it's typical, will last less than 15 minutes. The trustee will briefly go over your forms with you. The judge isn't present. The trustee is likely to be most interested in the fairness of your plan and your ability to make the payments you have proposed.

When the trustee is finished, any creditors who showed up are given a chance to question you. Often, secured creditors come, especially if they have any objections to the plan—for example, that your plan isn't feasible, you are taking too long to pay your arrears on a secured debt or the value you assigned the collateral is wrong. An unsecured creditor who is receiving very little under your plan might show up, too, if that creditor thinks you can cut your expenses and increase your disposable income.

At the end of the hearing, be ready to negotiate with the creditors. If you agree to make changes to accommodate their objections, you must submit a modified plan.

b. Confirmation Hearing

The confirmation hearing is the hearing at which the court approves or rejects your proposed repayment plan. The trustee or a creditor may raise objections, and often does. Typical objections include the following.

The plan is not submitted in good faith. Probably the most common objection raised is that a Chapter 13 plan was not proposed in good faith. Bankruptcy rules do not define good faith, but bankruptcy courts generally look to see that you have not proposed a plan that obviously will be impossible for you to meet. If you feel confident that you are filing your papers with the honest intention of getting back on your feet and can make the payments under the plan, you probably can overcome a "good faith" objection. When creditors pursue good faith objections, most bankruptcy courts look at the following kinds of factors:

- *How often you have filed for bankruptcy.* Filing multiple bankruptcies (file, dismiss, file, dismiss and file again) in and of itself does not show bad faith. If within one year, however, you've filed and dismissed two or more other bankruptcy cases, the court may find lack of good faith if there are inconsistencies in your papers or you cannot show that your circumstances have changed since the previous dismissal.

- *The accuracy of your bankruptcy papers and oral statements.* The court is likely to find a lack of good faith if you misrepresent your income, debts, expenses or assets, or you lie at the creditors' meeting.
- *Your efforts to repay your debts.* If you will pay your unsecured creditors less than the full amount that you owe, you will have to show the court that you are stretching as much as you can. The court will want to see that you are not living luxuriously and that you are making substantial efforts to pay your unsecured creditors.

The plan is not feasible. The second most likely objection is that your plan is not feasible—that is, you won't be able to make the payments or comply with the other terms of the plan. To overcome a feasibility objection, your monthly income must exceed your monthly expenses by at least enough to allow you to make payments required under Chapter 13 bankruptcy. (See Section A.2, above.)

The trustee or a creditor might also question your job stability, the likelihood that you'll incur extraordinary expenses and whether you have any outside sources of money. The court will likely deny confirmation on the ground that your plan isn't feasible if any of the following are true:

- Your business has been failing, but you've predicted a rebound and intend to use business income to make your plan payments.
- You propose making plan payments from the proceeds of the sale of certain property, but nothing points to the likelihood of a sale.
- Your plan includes a balloon payment (a large payment at the end), but you have not identified a source of money with which to make the payment.
- You've been convicted of a crime, and you have not convinced the bankruptcy court that you will stay out of jail.

The plan fails the best interest of the creditors test. Under your Chapter 13 repayment plan, you must pay your unsecured creditors at least as much as they would have received had you filed for Chapter 7 bankruptcy—that is, the value of your nonexempt property. (Exempt and nonexempt property are discussed in Chapters 4 and 5.) This is called the "best interest of the creditors" test.

If the trustee or a creditor raises this objection, you will have to provide documents showing the values of your nonexempt items of property, such as a recent appraisal of your house or a publication stating the value of an automobile of your make, model and year.

The plan unfairly discriminates. Chapter 13 bankruptcy is designed so that all unsecured creditors are paid the same percentage. You might be inclined to pay some more than others—for example 100% of a student loan that isn't dischargeable but only 35% on your credit cards. In this situation, the trustee or the credit card issuers are likely to object to your plan on the ground that they are unfairly being discriminated against.

Unlike a creditors' meeting, the confirmation hearing is run by the judge. The judge is most interested in your ability to make the payments under your plan, and will question you about that or about plan provisions that are unclear. After these questions, the judge will ask you if the objections have been resolved. If they haven't, the judge may ask the trustee or creditors to elaborate on their objections, ask you for any response and then make a ruling.

If the judge agrees with an objection, you will probably be allowed to submit a modified plan. But if it's obvious that Chapter 13 bankruptcy just isn't realistic for you—for example, you earn very little money to pay into a plan—the judge will order that your case be dismissed unless you can convert it to Chapter 7 bankruptcy before the date set for the dismissal.

c. Valuation Hearing

A valuation hearing may be requested by a creditor to determine the value of an item of collateral. This frequently comes up when you claim that an item of collateral, such as a car, is worth less than you owe and you want to pay only its value. If a creditor requests a valuation hearing, your confirmation hearing will be postponed, or the court will hold the valuation hearing immediately before the confirmation hearing.

d. Relief From Stay Hearing

A relief from stay hearing may be requested by a creditor who wants to pursue collection efforts against you. This could come up, for example, if you fall further behind on your mortgage or car payments after you file your bankruptcy papers.

e. Discharge Hearing

Discharge hearings used to occur frequently, at the end of cases. Today, because of the high number of bankruptcy filings, few judges require you to come to court for a discharge hearing. You'll probably just receive a letter from the court letting you know that your case is over and that any balance remaining on your dischargeable debts has been discharged.

At the back of this book is a checklist entitled, "Should I File For Bankruptcy?" As you finish each chapter, you'll be reminded to turn to the checklist to answer the questions that were raised by that chapter's discussion. Once you've read the entire book and have completed the checklist, you will have before you a summary of the major issues you face in deciding whether or not to file.

HISTORY OF BANKRUPTCY

In one form or another, debtors unable to pay their bills have been around for a long time. Not surprisingly, so has bankruptcy. Although scholars may differ as to its exact nature, some sort of debt relief was known even in Biblical times. (See Deuteronomy 15:1-2—"Every seventh year you shall practice remission of debts. This shall be the nature of the remission: Every creditor shall remit the due that he claims from his neighbor; he shall not dun his neighbor or kinsman.")

The first "modern" bankruptcy law was passed in England in 1542, under King Henry VIII, to give creditors remedies other than imprisonment against debtors who did not pay their bills. Under this law, debtors were considered quasi-criminals.

In 1570, during the reign of Queen Elizabeth I, England passed its second bankruptcy law:

- Only a creditor could commence a bankruptcy case—that is, bankruptcy was involuntary for the debtor.
- Only a merchant could be a debtor. Nonmerchants—ordinary people—were still being thrown in jail.
- During the bankruptcy case, a bankruptcy commissioner, much like the modern trustee, seized the bankrupt's assets, sold them and distributed them pro rata to the creditors.
- At the end of the case, any balance owed was not wiped out, so creditors could continue their collection efforts.

Over the next 100 or so years, the British Parliament made a few changes to this bankruptcy law, primarily to let the commissioner take more of the bankrupt's assets and to increase penalties for noncompliance. A 1604 amendment passed during the time of King James I permitted the debtor's ear to be cut off.

In 1705, Queen Anne and Parliament made sweeping changes:

- A cooperative bankrupt could have the unpaid balance of his debts wiped out.
- A cooperative bankrupt would also be entitled to keep certain property based on the total value of his assets.
- An uncooperative bankrupt who was defrauding his creditors could be put to death, although records indicate that only five debtors were put to death during the 115 years this provision existed.

The 1732 bankruptcy law, passed during the reign of King George II, had essentially the same provisions as the 1705 law—discharge and exemptions for cooperative debtor; death for fraudulent debtor—and still, bankruptcy was an involuntary proceeding brought by creditors against merchant debtors.

Neither the Articles of Confederation nor the U.S. Constitution contained specific provisions for bankruptcy—although the Constitution gives power to establish uniform bankruptcy laws to the Congress. Early independent America had no bankruptcy laws.

In 1800, Congress, by one vote, passed the first American bankruptcy law. It was very similar to Britain's 1732 act, although a fraudulent bankrupt could not be sentenced to death. It was repealed three years later.

Congress tried again in 1841, after the abolishment of debtors' prisons. The new act allowed for both merchant and nonmerchant debtors. Debtors could keep basic property items, although there were limits on what debts could be wiped out. Debtors as well as creditors could file cases. The creation of debtor filings—voluntary bankruptcies—was a watershed event. Thousands of debtors filed for bankruptcy, and creditors received very little. The act was repealed after two years.

Congress tried again in 1867. This law allowed for both merchant and nonmerchant debtors, and allowed voluntary and involuntary cases. Debtors had to take an oath of allegiance to the United States (this was just after the Civil War). This law lasted 11 years and was repealed because too many debtors were using it and creditors were getting little in return.

Modern American bankruptcy has its permanent beginning with the Bankruptcy Act of 1898. This law allowed both voluntary and involuntary cases, permitted debtors to keep certain items of property and removed most barriers for eliminating virtually all debts. One commentator of the time suggested Congress went too far in favoring debtors. He reminded them that bankruptcy was primarily a "commercial regulation," not a general debtor "jubilee" as provided in the Bible.

During the 1920s, the act was amended to add grounds to deny a bankruptcy and to add debts that could not be wiped out. In 1938, the Chandler Act saw the radical overhaul of American bankruptcy law. Although most of the changes affected business bankruptcies, the Chandler Act created Chapter XIII, the wage earners' plan.

The next—and last—major change came with the enactment of the Bankruptcy Act of 1978, the law that exists today. Congress almost annually considers legislation that would radically amend the current bankruptcy law. (See Chapter 11.)

2

Who Can File for Bankruptcy?

It's possible that bankruptcy is the right solution, but that you aren't eligible to file. For example, Chapter 7 bankruptcy isn't available to you if you received a Chapter 7 discharge within the previous six years; in addition, you cannot file for Chapter 13 bankruptcy if your debts exceed a certain amount. Your eligibility to file is something you should figure out sooner rather than later.

A. Chapter 7 Bankruptcy Eligibility Requirements

There are several basic eligibility requirements you must meet to file a consumer Chapter 7 bankruptcy (this term was defined in Chapter 1, Section A).

1. You Must Be an Individual (or Married Couple) or Small Business Person

To file a consumer Chapter 7 bankruptcy case, you must be an individual (or a husband and wife filing jointly) or a small business person. As a small business person, you can include all business debts on which you have personal liability. For example, if you operate your business as a sole proprietor or as a sole proprietor in partnership with your spouse, you or you and your spouse are personally liable for the debts of the business. For bankruptcy purposes, you are one and the same. You can include all of the business debts in your consumer Chapter 7 bankruptcy case.

Similarly, if you are a member of a business partnership, you can file for Chapter 7 bankruptcy as a consumer and include all business debts on which you are personally liable. Your partners will remain fully liable for the debts you wipe out, however.

If you are a member of a business partnership, you'll probably want to consult a small business lawyer before you file for bankruptcy. Your obligation to your partners may be governed by any buy-sell agreement requiring you to terminate your partnership interest before filing for bankruptcy. If you don't follow that agreement or any other understanding you and your partners have, you probably will be putting the partnership property at risk and may find that your partners (or ex-partners) ask that the bankruptcy court lift the automatic stay so they can file a lawsuit against you.

You cannot file a consumer Chapter 7 bankruptcy case on behalf of a corporation, limited liability company or partnership. In that situation, you must file a business Chapter 7 bankruptcy, which is beyond the scope of this book.

2. You Haven't Received a Previous Bankruptcy Discharge

You cannot file for Chapter 7 bankruptcy if you obtained a discharge of your debts in a Chapter 7 bankruptcy or Chapter 13 bankruptcy case begun within the past six years. The six-year period runs from the date you filed the earlier bankruptcy case, not the date of your discharge.

Example: On June 14, 1997, you filed a Chapter 7 bankruptcy. You received your discharge on November 2, 1997. You've fallen on hard times again and are considering filing another Chapter 7 case. You cannot file before June 15, 2003. You can file for Chapter 13 bankruptcy at any time, however.

3. You Aren't Barred by a Previous Bankruptcy Dismissal

You cannot file for Chapter 7 bankruptcy if a previous bankruptcy case was dismissed within the past 180 days because you violated a court order, the court ruled that your filing was fraudulent or an abuse of the bankruptcy system or you requested the dismissal after a creditor asked the court to lift the automatic stay.

Example: You filed for Chapter 7 bankruptcy on February 12, 2001 after your landlord started eviction proceedings. A week after you filed, your landlord filed a motion with the bankruptcy court to have the automatic stay lifted to continue the eviction proceedings. You dismissed your case. You've found a new place to live, but your debt problems haven't gone away and you want to refile. You must wait until at least 180 days before filing again—that is, until August 12, 2001.

4. You Couldn't Pay Off Your Debts in a Chapter 13 Bankruptcy

A bankruptcy judge can, and increasingly judges do, prohibit you from pursuing a Chapter 7 bankruptcy case if the judge decides that you have enough assets or income to repay most of your debts either in a Chapter 13 bankruptcy or outside of bankruptcy altogether. In that situation, the judge is likely to suggest that you voluntarily convert your case to Chapter 13 bankruptcy. If you don't the judge may dismiss your case.

A judge isn't likely to suggest conversion of your case or order dismissal unless both of the following are true:

- you have an adequate and steady income, and
- with a modification of lifestyle, you could pay off all or most of your debts over three to five years.

5. You Have Been Honest With Your Creditors

Bankruptcy is geared toward the honest debtor who got in too deep and needs the help of the bankruptcy court to get a fresh start. Your Chapter 7 bankruptcy case may be challenged or dismissed if you have played fast and loose with your creditors or you try to do so with the bankruptcy court. Certain activities are red flags to bankruptcy courts and trustees. If you have engaged in any of them during the past year and are caught, your eligibility to file a Chapter 7 bankruptcy case is likely to be challenged. The no-no's include:

- unloading assets or cash to your friends or relatives to hide them from your creditors or the bankruptcy court
- incurring debts (other than for necessities) when you were clearly broke and had no ability or intention of repaying them
- concealing property from your spouse during a divorce proceeding, and
- lying about your income or debts on a credit application—such as stating your income as $48,000 when you earned only $18,000.

These activities cast a suspicion of fraud over your entire bankruptcy case.

B.   Chapter 13 Bankruptcy Eligibility Requirements

Like Chapter 7 bankruptcy, Chapter 13 bankruptcy has several important eligibility requirements.

1.   Businesses Can't File for Chapter 13 Bankruptcy

To file a Chapter 13 bankruptcy case, you must be an individual (or a husband and wife filing jointly). If you own your own small business, you can include all business debts on which you have personal liability. You would have to file your case in your name, however, and not the name of the business—because a business cannot file for Chapter 13 bankruptcy. You will list all fictitious business names or DBAs ("doing business as") that you've used as a sole proprietor on your bankruptcy papers.

As with Chapter 7 bankruptcy, if you operate your business as a sole proprietor or as a sole proprietor in partnership with your spouse, you or you and your spouse are personally liable for the debts of the business. For bankruptcy purposes, you are one and the same. You can include all of the business debts in your Chapter 13 bankruptcy case. You can also include the debts you are personally liable for as a member of a business partnership. There is one exception: stockbrokers and commodity brokers cannot file a Chapter 13 bankruptcy case, even if just to include personal (nonbusiness) debts.

You cannot file a Chapter 13 bankruptcy on behalf of a corporation, limited liability company or partnership. If you want to file a reorganization bankruptcy in that situation, you must file a business Chapter 11 bankruptcy, which is beyond the scope of this book.

2. You Must Have Stable and Regular Income

You must have stable and regular income to be eligible for Chapter 13 bankruptcy. That doesn't mean you must earn the same amount every month. But the income must be steady—that is, likely to continue—and it must be periodic—weekly, monthly, quarterly, semi-annual, seasonal or even annual. You can use the following income to fund a Chapter 13 plan:

- regular wages or salary
- income from self-employment
- wages from seasonal work
- commissions from sales or other work
- pension payments
- Social Security benefits (although a court might rule that Social Security payments do not constitute regular income to fund a Chapter 13 plan)
- disability or workers' compensation benefits
- unemployment benefits, strike benefits and the like
- public benefits (welfare payments)
- child support or alimony you receive
- royalties and rents
- gifts of money from relatives or friends, and
- proceeds from selling property, especially if selling property is your primary business.

3. You Must Have Disposable Income

For you to qualify for Chapter 13 bankruptcy, you devise a plan under which you devote all of your disposable income—what's left over after you pay your necessary expenses—toward paying off your debts. The total amount of your payments under your plan must be at least equal to what your creditors would have received had you filed for Chapter 7 bankruptcy—that is, the value of your nonexempt property. (Exempt property is the property you would be allowed to keep if you file a Chapter 7 case. Exempt property is explained in Chapters 4 and 5.)

Bankruptcy law requires that you pay all your disposable income into your Chapter 13 plan for a minimum of 36 months unless you can pay off all of your debts in less time. On the other hand, if making 36 monthly payments will not be enough to repay the minimum amount required by the court (the minimum amount you must pay in a Chapter 13 bankruptcy is discussed in Chapter 1, Section A.2.), you will have to do one of the following:

- Ask the court to approve a plan that lasts more than 36 months. The court can authorize a plan of up to 60 months (five years).
- Increase your monthly disposable income, usually by decreasing your expenses, so that more money is distributed to your creditors each month.

The income you use to repay creditors need not be wages. You can use benefits, pension payments, investment income or receipts as an independent contractor. Some courts let you use the proceeds of the sale of a substantial item of property—such as your house or business—to augment your wages or other source of income. If you haven't already taken any steps to begin selling the property, however, it's unlikely a court will allow you to include the proceeds of the sale when totaling up your income. If you want to use the proceeds from the sale of property, make sure the property is listed for sale with a broker. Better yet, show the court an accepted offer on the property or an escrow closing date.

To determine if your disposable income is high enough to fund a Chapter 13 plan, you must create a reasonable monthly budget. If you are not proposing to repay 100% of your unsecured debts and the court, the trustee or a creditor thinks your budget is too generous—that is, it includes expenses other than necessities—your budget will be challenged. On the flip side, if you aren't realistic about what it costs to live—that is, you've understated your expenses so that you produce enough income to fund a plan—your creditors or the trustee is likely to object on the ground that your plan isn't feasible.

4. Your Debts Must Not Be Too High

You do not qualify for Chapter 13 bankruptcy if your secured debts exceed $807,750 or your unsecured debts are more than $269,250. If you need help figuring out which of your debts are secured and which are unsecured, keep reading.

a. Secured Debts

A debt is secured if you stand to lose specific property if you don't make your payments to the creditor. Most secured debts are created when you sign loan papers giving a creditor a security interest in your property—such as a home loan or car loan. But a debt might also be secured if a creditor has filed a lien, or notice of claim, against your property.

Here is a list of common secured debts:

- **Mortgages** (called deeds of trust in some states), which are loans to buy or refinance a house or other real estate. If you fail to pay, the lender can foreclose on your house.

- **Home equity loans** (second mortgages) from banks or finance companies, such as loans to do work on your house. If you fail to pay, the lender can foreclose on the your house.

- **Loans for cars, boats, tractors, motorcycles or RVs.** If you fail to pay, the lender can repossess the vehicle.

- **Store charges with a security agreement.** Almost all store purchases on credit cards are unsecured. Some stores, notably Sears and J.C. Penney, however, claim to retain a security interest in all hard goods (durable goods) purchased or make customers sign security agreements when they use their store charge card.

- **Personal loans from banks, credit unions or finance companies.** Often you must pledge valuable personal property, such as a paid-off motor vehicle, as collateral, which can be repossessed if you don't make the payments.

- **Judicial liens.** A judicial lien can be imposed on your property only after somebody sues you and wins a money judgment against you. In most states, the judgment creditor then must record (file) the judgment with the county or state; the recorded judgment creates the lien on your real estate and some personal property in that county or state.

- **Statutory liens.** Some liens are created automatically by law. For example, in most states when you hire someone to work on your house, the worker or supplier of materials automatically gets a mechanic's lien (sometimes called a materialman's or contractor's lien) on the house if you don't pay.

- **Tax liens.** If you owe money to the IRS or other taxing authority, the debt is secured if the agency has recorded a lien against your property.

b. Unsecured Debts

An unsecured debt is any debt for which you haven't pledged collateral and for which the creditor has not filed a lien against you. If the debt is unsecured, the creditor is not entitled to repossess or seize any of your property if you don't pay.

Most debts are unsecured. Some of the common ones are:

- credit and charge card (Visa, MasterCard, American Express, Discover and the like) purchases and cash advances
- department store credit card purchases, unless the store retains a security interest in the items you buy or requires you to sign a security agreement
- gasoline company credit card purchases
- back rent
- medical bills
- alimony and child support
- student loans
- utility bills
- loans from friends or relatives, unless you signed a promissory note secured by some property you own
- health club dues
- lawyers' and accountants' bills

- church or synagogue dues, and
- union dues.

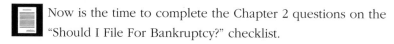 Now is the time to complete the Chapter 2 questions on the "Should I File For Bankruptcy?" checklist.

Will I Wipe Out My Debts?

The primary reason why a person files for bankruptcy is to get rid of debts—either immediately (in a Chapter 7 bankruptcy) or over time (in a Chapter 13 bankruptcy). This chapter explains which debts can't be discharged (eliminated) in a Chapter 7 bankruptcy, and how much you might still owe after your Chapter 13 bankruptcy is over.

A. Debts Not Dischargeable in Chapter 7 Bankruptcy

Under the bankruptcy laws, several categories of debts may turn out to be nondischargeable. Some debts are never dischargeable, unless you prove that the debt fits within a narrow exception to the general rule. Other debts are always dischargeable, unless the creditor files an objection in the bankruptcy court and convinces the court to rule that the debt isn't.

ARE SECURED DEBTS DISCHARGEABLE?

Secured debts are linked to specific items of property, called collateral. The property guarantees payment of the debt. Common secured debts include personal loans from banks, car loans and home loans.

Bankruptcy eliminates your personal liability for your secured debts—the creditor can't sue you for the debt itself. But bankruptcy doesn't eliminate the creditor's lien on the secured property. To eliminate the lien, you'll have to give the secured property to the creditor or pay the creditor its current value or the debt amount, whichever is less. In a few situations, you can file papers with the court to request that a lien be wiped out. And if you wish, you can agree to have the debt survive bankruptcy, keep the collateral and make payments under the original loan agreement.

---

1. Debts Not Dischargeable Unless an Exception Applies

Several kinds of debts cannot be discharged unless you show the bankruptcy court that the debt falls within an exception to the general rule declaring the debt nondischargeable.

a. Debts or Creditors You Don't List

For a debt to be discharged in your bankruptcy case, the creditor must know about your case. Creditors usually hear of a bankruptcy filing from the trustee, who sends a notice to all creditors listed in your bankruptcy papers. If the official notice fails to reach the creditor for some reason beyond your control—for example, because the post office errs or the creditor changed locations without leaving a forwarding address—the debt will be discharged.

But if you forget to list a creditor on your bankruptcy papers or carelessly misstate a creditor's identity or address, the creditor won't be notified by the court. If that happens, the debt won't be discharged unless the creditor knew of your bankruptcy through other means, such as a letter or phone call from you.

If at any time during the bankruptcy case you discover that you left a creditor or debt off your bankruptcy papers, you can amend them. And if you don't discover the omission until after your case is over, you can make a request to the court to reopen your case to amend your papers and have the loan discharged. Your request is likely to be granted if not a lot of time has passed (less than a year) since your case ended and your case was a no-asset case—meaning that no money was paid to your creditors during your bankruptcy.

b. Student Loans

Most student loans are nondischargeable—you'll still have to repay them after bankruptcy. But the bankruptcy court may let you discharge a student loan if repaying your loan would cause you undue hardship. In determining undue hardship, bankruptcy courts look to three factors. If you can show that all factors are present, the court is likely to grant you an undue hardship discharge of your student loan.

- *Poverty.* Based on your current income and expenses, you cannot maintain a minimal living standard and repay the loan.
- *Persistence.* Your current financial condition is likely to continue indefinitely—that is, your situation is hopeless or virtually hopeless.
- *Good faith.* You've made a good-faith effort to repay your debt. You're not likely to be granted a hardship discharge if you file for

bankruptcy immediately after getting out of school or if you haven't looked extensively for employment.

Courts rarely allow student loans to be discharged on hardship grounds. They take the position that Congress wants student loans to be repaid absent exceptional circumstances. And sometimes, even if a court finds that it would be a hardship to repay the entire debt, the court allows only a portion of it to be discharged.

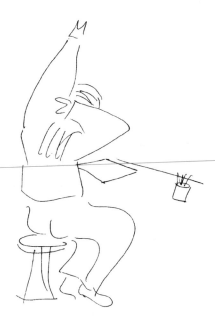

SPECIAL RULES FOR HEAL AND PLUS LOANS

HEAL. The dischargeability of Health Education Assistance Loans (HEAL loans) is governed by the federal HEAL Act, not bankruptcy law. Under the HEAL Act, to discharge a loan, you must show that the loan became due more than seven years past, and that repaying it would not merely be a hardship, but would impose an unconscionable burden on your life.

PLUS. Parental Loans for Students (PLUS Loans) are granted to a parent to finance a child's education. Even though the parent does not receive the education, if the parent files for bankruptcy, the loan is treated like any other student loan. The parents must meet the undue hardship test to discharge the loan.

---

c. Taxes

As a general rule, recent federal, state and local taxes aren't dischargeable in Chapter 7 bankruptcy. Although there are some exceptions, these exceptions seldom apply in practice. And even if they do, the taxing authority will probably be able to enforce any tax lien that has been placed on your property. Here are the specifics.

Income taxes. You can discharge debts for federal income taxes in Chapter 7 bankruptcy only if all of these five conditions are true:

1. You filed a legitimate (nonfraudulent) tax return.
2. The liability is for a tax return (not a Substitute For Return) actually filed at least two years before you file for bankruptcy.
3. The tax return was due at least three years before you file for bankruptcy.
4. The IRS has not assessed against you liability for the taxes within the 240 days (eight months) before you file for bankruptcy. You're probably safe if you do not receive a formal notice of assessment of federal taxes from the IRS during the 240 days before filing for bankruptcy.

5. The IRS has not recorded a tax lien against your property. If all other conditions are met, the taxes may be discharged, but the lien will remain after your bankruptcy, giving the IRS a way to collect. This means that the discharge isn't really a discharge, because you'll have to pay off the lien before you can transfer clear title to your property.

    Also, if you borrowed money or used your credit card to pay taxes that would otherwise be nondischargeable, you cannot eliminate the loan or credit card debt in bankruptcy. In other words, you can't turn your nondischargeable tax debt into a dischargeable tax debt by paying it on your credit card.

    Property taxes. Property taxes aren't dischargeable unless they became due more than a year before you file for bankruptcy. But even if your personal liability for paying the property tax out of your pocket is discharged, the tax lien on your property is unaffected. From a practical standpoint, this discharge is no discharge at all, because you'll have to pay off the lien before you can transfer clear title to the property.

    Other taxes. Other types of taxes that aren't dischargeable are business-related: payroll taxes, excise taxes and customs duties. Sales, use and poll taxes are also probably not dischargeable. If you owe any of these types of tax debts, see a bankruptcy attorney.

d. Child Support and Alimony

An obligation that has been labeled child support, alimony or something similar is nondischargeable. Some other debts may also be considered nondischargeable child support or alimony even though they are called something else. The most common are certain marital debts—the debts one spouse agreed to or was ordered to pay when a couple divorced.

Often, a spouse who is paying alimony agrees at the time of a divorce to pay more than half of the marital debts, in exchange for a lower alimony obligation. If that spouse later files for bankruptcy, a portion of the marital debts may really be alimony and considered nondischargeable. Similarly, one spouse may have agreed to pay some of the other spouse's or children's future living expenses (shelter, clothing, health insurance, transportation) in exchange for a lower support obligation. The obligations to pay the future living expenses may be treated as support owed to the other spouse and considered nondischargeable.

 Some divorce-related (nonsupport) debts may be declared nondischargeable if the nonfiling ex-spouse objects. See Section A.2.d, below.)

e. Fines, Penalties and Restitution

You cannot discharge fines, penalties or restitution that a federal, state or local government has imposed to punish you for violating a law. Examples include:

- fines imposed for infractions, misdemeanors or felonies
- fines imposed by a judge for contempt of court
- fines imposed by a government agency for violating agency regulations
- surcharges imposed by a court or agency for enforcement of a law, and
- restitution orders to be paid to economically injured victims imposed in criminal cases.

f. Court Fees

You cannot discharge a fee imposed by a court for the filing of a case, motion, complaint or appeal, or for other costs and expenses assessed with respect to such court filing. The law targets prisoners who attempt to discharge court fees, especially fees related to appeals, but its scope is much greater.

g. Intoxicated Driving Debts

Debts for the death of, or personal injury to, someone resulting from your driving while illegally intoxicated by alcohol or drugs aren't dischargeable. Even if you are sued and the judge or jury finds you liable but doesn't specifically find that you were intoxicated, the judgment against you won't be discharged if you were, in fact, intoxicated.

Debts for property damage resulting from your intoxicated driving are dischargeable.

h. Debts You Couldn't Discharge in a Previous Bankruptcy

If a bankruptcy court dismissed a previous bankruptcy case because of your fraud or other bad acts (misfeasance), you cannot discharge any debts that would have been discharged in the earlier bankruptcy had the filing been allowed. This rule doesn't affect debts incurred since the date you filed the earlier bankruptcy case.

Example: You filed for Chapter 7 bankruptcy in 1997, during a really rough time in your life. You had received a Chapter 7 discharge in 1994, which made you ineligible to file for Chapter 7 again before 2000, so you used a phony Social Security number when you filed in 1997. The court quickly discovered your ruse and dismissed your case. Luckily for you, you were not prosecuted for fraud. You want to file a Chapter 7 case again. You can because six years have passed since you received your 1994 discharge. You won't be able to discharge any of the debts you listed in your 1997 case, however.

2. Debts Discharged Unless the Creditor Objects

Four types of debts will be discharged unless the creditor objects during the bankruptcy proceedings and proves that the debt fits in one of the following categories.

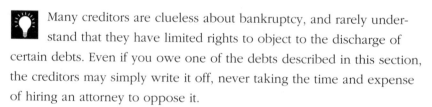 Many creditors are clueless about bankruptcy, and rarely understand that they have limited rights to object to the discharge of certain debts. Even if you owe one of the debts described in this section, the creditors may simply write it off, never taking the time and expense of hiring an attorney to oppose it.

a. Debts From Fraud

This category has several subcategories; to be nondischargeable, a debt must fit within at least one.

Debts from intentionally fraudulent behavior. If a creditor can show that a debt arose because of your dishonest act, and that the debt wouldn't have arisen had you been honest, the court will probably not let you discharge the debt. These are common examples:

- You wrote a check for something and stopped payment on it after changing your mind and deciding not to pay.
- You wrote a check against insufficient funds but assured the merchant that the check was good.
- You rented or borrowed an expensive item and claimed it was yours to get a loan.
- You got a loan by telling the lender you'd pay it back, when you had no intention of doing so.

For a debt to be nondischargeable under this section, your deceit must be intentional, and the creditor must have relied on your deceit in extending credit.

Debts from a false written statement about your financial condition. If a creditor proves that you incurred a debt because of a false written statement you made, the debt isn't dischargeable. Here are the rules:

- The false statement must be written—for instance, made in a credit application, rental application or resume.
- The false statement must have been material—that is, a potentially significant factor in the creditor's decision to extend you credit. The two most common materially false statements are omitting debts and overstating income.
- The false statement must relate to your financial condition or the financial condition of an "insider"—a person close to you or a business entity with which you're associated.
- The creditor must have relied on the false statement, and the reliance must have been reasonable.
- You must have intended to deceive the creditor. This is extremely hard to prove based simply on your behavior. The creditor would have to show outrageous behavior on your part, such as adding a "0" to your income (claiming $180,000 when you make only $18,000) on a credit application.

Recent debts for luxuries. Bankruptcy law presumes that if you ran up debts of more than $1,075 to one creditor for luxury goods or services within 60 days before filing for bankruptcy, you intended to cheat the creditor or subvert the bankruptcy process.

Recent cash advances. If you obtained cash advances totaling more than $1,075 under an open-ended consumer credit plan fewer than 60 days before you filed for bankruptcy, the debt is nondischargeable. "Open-ended" means there's no date when the debt must be repaid, but rather, as with most credit cards, you may take forever to repay the debt as long as you pay a minimum amount each month.

Increasingly, banks are claiming that debtors incur credit card debt fraudulently—that is, without the intent to repay—and that therefore they should not be allowed to discharge those debts. The specific situations in which credit card debts give rise to fraud are explained just above. Additional information on credit card issuers' attempts to have credit card debt declared nondischargeable because of fraud is explained in Chapter 6, Section D.

b. Debts From Willful and Malicious Acts

If the act that caused a debt was willful and malicious (an act which intends to produce a specific injury), the debt isn't dischargeable if the creditor successfully objects. Most creditors don't object.

Generally, crimes that injure people or property are considered willful and malicious acts. An example is stabbing someone with a knife because you're angry. Your liability for the injury or damage the victim sustained will probably be ruled nondischargeable if the victim-creditor objects during your bankruptcy case. Other acts sometimes considered to be willful and malicious include:

- kidnapping someone
- deliberately causing extreme anxiety, fear or shock
- libel or slander, and
- prohibited activities of a landlord to evict a tenant, such as removing a door or changing the locks.

c. Debts From Embezzlement, Larceny or Breach of Fiduciary Duty

A debt incurred as a result of embezzlement, larceny or breach of fiduciary duty is nondischargeable if the creditor successfully objects to its discharge.

Embezzlement is taking property entrusted to you for another and using it for yourself. Larceny is another word for theft. Breach of fiduciary duty is the failure to live up to a duty of trust you owe someone, based on a relationship where you're required to manage property or money for another, or where your relationship is a close and confidential one. Common fiduciary relationships are:

- among business partners
- attorney and client
- estate executor and beneficiary
- guardian and ward, and
- husband and wife.

d. Debts From a Divorce Decree or Marital Settlement Agreement

Any nonsupport debt arising from a separation agreement or divorce, or in connection with a marital settlement agreement, divorce decree or other court order, can be considered nondischargeable. (Support debts are automatically nondischargeable. See Section A.1.d, above.) Your ex-spouse or child must challenge the discharge of the debt in the bankruptcy court. The court will allow the debt to be discharged unless:

- you have the ability to pay the debt from income or property not reasonably necessary for your support and not reasonably necessary for you to continue, preserve and operate a business, or
- discharging the debt would result in a detriment to your former spouse or child that would outweigh the benefit you would receive by the discharge.

It's easy to confuse this category with nondischargeable alimony or child support (Section A.1.d, above.) That's because not all separation agreements or divorce decrees specify the differences. For example, if you agreed to pay the marital debts in exchange for your spouse giving up (waiving) her full share of the marital property and alimony, are the marital debts you agreed to pay marital debts (as meant by this section) or in the nature of support (as meant in Section A.1.d)? To the extent that the debts are in exchange for waiving alimony, they probably are "in the nature of support" and are not dischargeable. To the extent they cover the division of marital debts and property, they fall into this category.

B. Debts You Will Still Owe When Your Chapter 13 Bankruptcy Is Over

It is possible that you will still owe money to some of your creditors when your Chapter 13 bankruptcy case is over. The debts described in Section A.1, above, cannot be discharged in any kind of bankruptcy case—Chapter 7 or Chapter 13. This means that if you do not pay them in full through your plan, you will owe a balance at the end of your case. If the debt was one on which the creditor was entitled to interest (such as a student loan or tax debt), you'll owe more than the unpaid balance. The creditor can and will probably tack on interest that stopped accruing during your Chapter 13 case.

The debts described in Section A.2, above, do not have to be paid in full in a Chapter 13 bankruptcy. (To refresh your memory on what debts are paid in full, see Chapter 1, Section A.2.) These are paid like other unsecured debts—such as credit cards and medical bills. If you don't pay them back in full, the balance is wiped out at the end of your case under what is referred to as Chapter 13 bankruptcy's "superdischarge."

C. Bankruptcy and Codebtors

Debts for which you have a codebtor raise some tricky issues. Let's look at the different kinds of codebtors and what your bankruptcy filing might mean.

1. Cosigners and Guarantors

If the underlying debt for which you have a cosigner or guarantor is dischargeable, your codebtor will get stuck owing the bill if you file for Chapter 7 bankruptcy and wipe out the debt.

If you want to file for Chapter 7 bankruptcy but don't want to stick it to a cosigner or guarantor, you can agree with the creditor as a part of your bankruptcy case to reaffirm the debt—that is, to be fully liable for it when your bankruptcy ends.

If you file for Chapter 13 bankruptcy, you can include the cosigned or guaranteed debt as part of your repayment plan, and your codebtor will not be pursued during your bankruptcy case. If you can, pay the debt in full during your case. If you don't, you will be entitled to discharge whatever balance remains when your case is over, assuming the debt is otherwise dischargeable in a Chapter 13 bankruptcy. But in that situation, the creditor can go after the codebtor for the balance.

BANKRUPTCY AND PREFERENCES

If you file for Chapter 7 bankruptcy and have a codebtor who is a relative, close friend or business associate, it's possible that she could be stuck owing more than just the amount that you discharge. If you made payments to the creditors on the debt during the year before filing for bankruptcy, the *codebtor* may owe the bankruptcy court the total amount of what you paid during that year.

That's because when you file for bankruptcy, the bankruptcy trustee will look to see if you made any payments to creditors within the 90 days before filing—within one year of filing if those payments were to, or for the benefit of, a relative or close business associate. These payments are called preferences and are not permitted, because you are not allowed to single out certain creditors for special treatment. The bankruptcy trustee can demand that the creditor (including your codebtor) give the money back. As illogical as this sounds, courts have upheld the right of bankruptcy trustees to ask codebtors to repay the entire amount to the court so that the money can be distributed pro rata to all creditors.

---

2. Spouse

Most married couples file for Chapter 7 bankruptcy together because their debts are joint. If, however, you are in a relatively new marriage, have not accumulated any joint (marital) property and want to get rid of separate (premarital) debts, you are probably safe filing alone. In addition, you may want to file alone if any of the following are true:

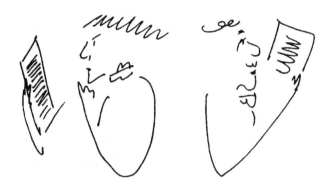

- **Your spouse owns separate, valuable property, such as a second home.** Your spouse would probably lose it to the bankruptcy court.

- **You and your spouse own a house in tenancy by the entirety.** This form of property ownership is available to married couples in Delaware, the District of Columbia, Hawaii, Maryland, Michigan, Missouri, North Carolina, Ohio, Pennsylvania, Tennessee, Vermont, Virginia and Wyoming. If one spouse files for bankruptcy, that spouse's creditors (and therefore the bankruptcy court) cannot take tenancy by the entirety property. If both spouses file, however, tenancy by the entirety property will probably be taken to pay the creditors.

- **You and your spouse have separated.** In such a situation, filing alone makes sense unless you haven't yet allocated debts and divided property.

- **You live in a community property state.** In community property states, virtually all debts incurred during marriage are considered community, or jointly owed. Under bankruptcy law, if only one spouse files for Chapter 7 bankruptcy in a community property state, the other spouse's share of the community debts is also discharged. In other words, the nonfiling spouse gets the benefit of the filing spouse's discharge with respect to the community debts. If one spouse did not want to file—for example, that spouse separately owns valuable nonexempt property—the other spouse could file alone and wipe out all community debts for both spouses. The community property states are Arizona, California, Idaho, Louisiana, Nevada, New Mexico, Texas, Washington and Wisconsin.

In a Chapter 13 bankruptcy, it rarely makes sense for only one spouse to file. The filing spouse must list the income, expenses and property of both spouses, and the bankruptcy case will have an impact on both spouses.

Only if you are separated from your spouse, have divided your property, agreed to pay the jointly incurred marital debts and have otherwise ended your financial entanglements (other than paying or receiving alimony or child support) should a married person file for Chapter 13 bankruptcy alone.

3. Business Partner

The effect of your bankruptcy filing on your business partners is discussed in Chapter 2, Sections A.1 and B.1.

 Now is the time to complete the Chapter 3 questions on the "Should I File For Bankruptcy?" checklist.

Will I Lose My House or Apartment?

O ne of the biggest worries you may face in considering filing for bankruptcy is the possible loss of your home, whether you own or rent. Take a deep breath and understand that the bankruptcy system is not designed to put you out on the street. If you're current on your house or rent payments and you can continue to afford them, you're at risk of losing your home only if you have equity in your home (defined below) above the exemption amount for your state (again, defined below). If you're behind but you can now afford to make your payments, you might be able to get back on track through bankruptcy. And if you can't afford your payments, bankruptcy can give you the breathing room to deal with the inevitable—finding a new place to live.

Read Section A if you're a homeowner; read Section B if you rent.

A. Home Ownership and Filing for Bankruptcy

Keeping your home in bankruptcy will depend on a number of factors— whether you are current or behind on your mortgage payments, the state in which you live and whether you file a Chapter 7 bankruptcy or a Chapter 13 bankruptcy. There are two general rules:

- If you are current on your mortgage payments, whether or not you will lose your house in a Chapter 7 bankruptcy depends on the amount of equity you have in the property and the amount of any homestead exemption to which you are entitled. ("Equity" and "homestead exemption" are defined in Section A.1., just below.) If you file for Chapter 13 bankruptcy, you will not lose your house as long as you continue to make your mortgage payments.

- If you are behind on your mortgage payments, you will almost certainly lose your house if you file a Chapter 7 bankruptcy. Your mortgage lender will ask the bankruptcy court to lift the automatic stay (the court order that bars creditors from trying to collect their debts), and the court will probably grant the request, allowing the mortgage lender to begin or resume foreclosure proceedings. In a Chapter 13 bankruptcy, you will not lose your house if you immediately resume making the regular payments called for under your agreement and repay your missed mortgage payments through your plan.

1. If You Are Current on Your Mortgage Payments

As mentioned, in a Chapter 7 bankruptcy, if you are current on your mortgage payments, you might still lose your house unless the homestead exemption available to you protects your equity. Your equity is the difference between the market value of your house and the debt against it.

a. How Much Is Your Equity?

If you don't know the current market value of your house, ask the real estate broker familiar with your neighborhood (such as the one you used when you bought your house) for an appraisal. There shouldn't be a charge for this.

Possible debts against your house include (these terms are defined in Chapter 2, Section B.4):

- the balance owed on any loan you took out to buy your house or to refinance your purchase (called a mortgage or deed of trust loan)
- the balance owed on any second (or third) mortgage
- the balance owed on any home equity loan or line of credit, and
- tax, judicial and other liens recorded by someone who claims you owe him or her money.

If the total amount of debt against your house is *more* than its market value, you have no equity and aren't at risk of losing the house as long as you keep current on your payments. Of course, in this situation you may consider your house to be an albatross, in which case you can use bankruptcy to get rid of it by "surrendering" your house to your creditors.

If the total amount of debt against your house is *less* than the market value, the bankruptcy trustee will want to take the house, sell it, use the proceeds to first pay off the mortgage lenders and any other lienholders and then use the rest to pay out some money to your unsecured creditors. The trustee won't be able to do this, however, if a homestead exemption entitles you to all (or most) of the equity. In that situation, after the trustee pays off the mortgage lenders and other lienholders, you would be entitled to your exemption before your unsecured creditors are paid. If there's nothing (or very little) left over for the unsecured creditors, there's no reason for the trustee to sell the house.

Example: The real estate broker you used when you bought your house told you that it is currently worth $300,000. You owe your mortgage lender $200,000 and the IRS (which has issued a Notice of Federal Tax Lien) $35,000. The equity in your house is $65,000 ($300,000 - $200,000 - $35,000). If the homestead exemption available to you is significantly less than $65,000, you are at risk of losing your house. The bankruptcy trustee will probably sell your house, pay off the mortgage lender and the IRS, reimburse himself for the cost of selling your house (as much as $10,000), give you the amount of the exemption (if there even is one) and use the rest of the proceeds to pay to your unsecured creditors. If your state homestead exemption is $65,000 or more, however, you shouldn't lose your house in Chapter 7 bankruptcy (as long as you are current on your payments). That's because if the bankruptcy trustee sold your home, after paying off the mortgage lender and IRS, you'd get your homestead exemption, which would eat up the rest of the money and leave nothing for the unsecured creditors. As explained in Chapter 1, one of the primary jobs of the bankruptcy trustee is to generate funds for unsecured creditors.

b. How Much Is Your Homestead Exemption?

Your homestead exemption is the amount of equity in your home you are entitled to keep if you file for Chapter 7 bankruptcy. That is one of the few universally applicable statements one can make about the homestead exemption. Another is that the amount of the homestead exemption varies tremendously from state to state. In fact, in a few states, it's not a monetary amount at all—it's based on your lot size. A handful of states have no homestead exemption at all. Some states are at the extreme other end—a very high or even unlimited amount of equity is protected by the homestead exemption. In a few states, the homestead exemption is based on both lot size and a monetary amount.

In 15 states and the District of Columbia, you must choose between two different amounts—one offered by your state and one offered under the federal Bankruptcy Code. (California debtors also must choose between different amounts, but both amounts are provided under state law.)

In a few states, you can increase the amount of the homestead exemption with a state wildcard exemption available to be put toward any property. Some states let a husband and wife filing jointly to double the amount.

One thing is consistent, however: to claim a homestead exemption, in virtually every state you must reside in the home as your primary residence when you file for bankruptcy. Homestead exemption laws do not protect second homes, vacation homes or other real estate in which you aren't living when you file.

State	Applicable Homestead Exemption
Alabama	You may exempt up to $5,000 of equity ($10,000 if a husband and wife file jointly) as long as the property does not exceed 160 acres.
Alaska	You may exempt up to $62,000 of equity.
Arizona	You may exempt up to $100,000 of equity.
Arkansas or Federal Exemption	Arkansas: Head of family may exempt an unlimited amount of equity as long as the property does not exceed 1/4 acre in a city, town or village, or 80 acres elsewhere. Head of family may exempt $2,500 of equity if the property is between 1/4–1 acre in a city, town or village, or between 80–160 acres elsewhere. There is no exemption for a head of family if the property exceeds 1 acre in a city, town or village, or 160 acres elsewhere. A person who is not a head of family may exempt up to $800 equity if single or $1,250 equity if married. Federal Exemption: You may exempt up to $15,000 of equity plus an $800 wildcard exemption.
California	System 1: You may exempt up to $50,000 of equity if you are single; up to $75,000 of equity if you are married; and up to $125,000 of equity if you are 65 or older, disabled or low income (single and earn under $15,000 or married and earn under $20,000). System 2: You may exempt up to $15,000 of equity plus an $800 wildcard exemption.
Colorado	You may exempt up to $30,000 of equity.
Connecticut or Federal Exemption	Connecticut: You may exempt up to $75,000 of equity plus a $1,000 wildcard exemption. Federal exemption: You may exempt up to $15,000 of equity plus an $800 wildcard exemption.
Delaware	No homestead exemption per se, however, if a spouse files for bankruptcy alone, a home in which the title is held as tenancy by the entirety (a form of title available only to married couples in a few states) may be exempt. If both spouses file, the tenancy by the entirety property is no longer exempt.
District of Columbia or Federal Exemption	District of Columbia: No homestead exemption per se, however, if a spouse files for bankruptcy alone, a home in which the title is held as tenancy by the entirety (a form of title available only to married couples in a few states) may be exempt. If both spouses file, the tenancy by the entirety property is no longer exempt. Federal exemption: You may exempt up to $15,000 of equity plus an $800 wildcard exemption

Florida	You may exempt an unlimited amount of equity as long as the property does not exceed $1/2$ acre in a municipality, or 160 acres elsewhere.
Georgia	You may exempt up to $5,000 of equity plus a $400 wildcard exemption.
Hawaii or Federal Exemption	Hawaii: Head of family or debtor over 65 may exempt up to $30,000 of equity as long as the property does not exceed 1 acre. Any other debtor may exempt up to $20,000 of equity as long as the property does not exceed 1 acre. Federal exemption: You may exempt up to $15,000 of equity plus an $800 wildcard exemption.
Idaho	You may exempt up to $50,000 of equity.
Illinois	You may exempt up to $7,500 of equity ($15,000 if a husband and wife file jointly).
Indiana	You may exempt up to $7,500 of equity plus a $4,000 wildcard exemption. In addition, if a spouse files for bankruptcy alone, a home in which the title is held as tenancy by the entirety (a form of title available only to married couples in a few states) may be exempt. If both spouses file, the tenancy by the entirety property is no longer exempt.
Iowa	You may exempt an unlimited amount of equity as long as the property does not exceed $1/2$ acre in a town or city, or 40 acres elsewhere.
Kansas	You may exempt an unlimited amount of equity as long as the property does not exceed 1 acre in a town or city, or 160 acres on a farm.
Kentucky	You may exempt up to $5,000 of equity plus a $1,000 wildcard exemtion.
Louisiana	You may exempt up to $15,000 of equity as long as the property does not exceed 160 acres on 1 tract, or on 2 tracts as long as there is a home on one tract and a field, garden or pasture on the other.
Maine	You may exempt up to $12,500 of equity ($25,000 if a husband and wife file jointly) plus a $400 wildcard exemption. If you are over 60 or disabled, you may exempt up to $60,000 of equity ($120,000 if a husband and wife file jointly) plus a $400 wildcard exemption.
Maryland	You may exempt up to $5,500 of equity by using the wildcard exemption. In addition, if a spouse files for bankruptcy alone, a home in which the title is held as tenancy by the entirety (a form of title available only to married couples in a few states) may be exempt. If both spouses file, the tenancy by the entirety property is no longer exempt.

Massachusetts or Federal Exemption	Massachusetts: You may exempt up to $100,000 of equity. If you are over 65 or disabled, you may exempt up to $200,000 of equity. Federal exemption:You may exempt up to $15,000 of equity plus an $800 wildcard exemption.
Michigan or Federal Exemption	Michigan: You may exempt up to $3,500 of equity as long as the property does not exceed 1 lot in a town, village or city, or 40 acres elsewhere. Federal exemption: You may exempt up to $15,000 of equity plus an $800 wildcard exemption.
Minnesota or Federal Exemption	Minnesota: You may exempt up to $200,000 of equity ($500,000 if the property is used primarily for agricultural purposes) as long as the property does not exceed $1/2$ acre in a city, or 160 acres elsewhere Federal exemption: You may exempt up to $15,000 of equity plus an $800 wildcard exemption.
Mississippi	You may exempt up to $75,000 of equity as long as the property does not exceed 160 acres.
Missouri	You may exempt up to $8,000 of equity ($1,000 if you live in a mobile home) plus a $400 wildcard exemption (head of family may claim a wildcard of $1,250 plus $250 per child).
Montana	You may exempt up to $60,000 of equity.
Nebraska	You may exempt up to $12,500 of equity as long as the property does not exceed 2 lots in a village or city, or 160 acres elsewhere.
Nevada	You may exempt up to $125,000 of equity.
New Hampshire or Federal Exemption	New Hampshire: You may exempt up to $30,000 of equity plus an $8,000 wildcard exemption. Federal exemption: You may exempt up to $15,000 of equity plus an $800 wildcard exemption.
New Jersey or Federal Exemption	New Jersey: No homestead exemption per se, however, if a spouse files for bankruptcy alone, a home in which the title is held as tenancy by the entirety (a form of title available only to married couples in a few states) may be exempt. If both spouses file, the tenancy by the entirety property is no longer exempt. Federal exemption: You may exempt up to $15,000 of equity plus an $800 wildcard exemption.
New Mexico or Federal Exemption	New Mexico: A debtor who is married or widowed or who supports another person may exempt up to $30,000 of equity. Federal exemption: You may exempt up to $15,000 of equity plus an $800 wildcard exemption.

New York	You may exempt up to $10,000 of equity ($20,000 if a husband and wife file jointly).
North Carolina	You may exempt up to $10,000 of equity. In addition, if a spouse files for bankruptcy alone, a home in which the title is held as tenancy by the entirety (a form of title available only to married couples in a few states) may be exempt. If both spouses file, the tenancy by the entirety property is no longer exempt.
North Dakota	You may exempt up to $80,000 of equity.
Ohio	You may exempt up to $5,000 of equity plus a $400 wildcard exemption. In addition, if a spouse files for bankruptcy alone, a home in which the title is held as tenancy by the entirety (a form of title available only to married couples in a few states) may be exempt. If both spouses file, the tenancy by the entirety property is no longer exempt.
Oklahoma	You may exempt an unlimited amount of equity as long as the property does not exceed $1/4$ acre in a city, town or village, or 160 acres elsewhere. You may exempt $5,000 of equity if the property exceeds $1/4$ acre in a city, town or village, or 160 acres elsewhere.
Oregon	You may exempt up to $25,000 of equity ($33,000 if a husband and wife file jointly) as long as the property does not exceed 1 block in a town or city, or 160 acres elsewhere. If you live in a mobile home and do not own the land on which your mobile home sits, you may exempt up to $23,000 of equity ($30,000 if a husband and wife file jointly).
Pennsylvania or Federal Exemption	Pennsylvania: No homestead exemption per se, but you may exempt up to $300 of equity by using the wildcard exemption. In addition, if a spouse files for bankruptcy alone, a home in which the title is held as tenancy by the entirety (a form of title available only to married couples in a few states) may be exempt. If both spouses file, the tenancy by the entirety property is no longer exempt. Federal exemption: You may exempt up to $15,000 of equity plus an $800 wildcard exemption.
Rhode Island or Federal Exemption	Rhode Island: No homestead exemption. Federal exemption: You may exempt up to $15,000 of equity plus an $800 wildcard exemption.
South Carolina	South Carolina: You may exempt up to $5,000 of equity ($10,000 if a husband and wife file jointly).
South Dakota	You may exempt an unlimited amount of equity as long as the property does not exceed 1 acre in a town, or 160 acres elsewhere.
Tennessee	You may exempt up to $5,000 of equity ($7,500 if a husband and wife file jointly).

Texas or Federal	Texas: You may exempt an unlimited amount of equity as long as the property does not exceed 10 acres in a town, village or city, or 100 acres (200 acres for a Exemption family) elsewhere. Federal exemption: You may exempt up to $15,000 of equity plus an $800 wildcard exemption.
Utah	You may exempt up to $10,000 of equity ($20,000 if a husband and wife file jointly).
Vermont or Federal Exemption	Vermont: You may exempt up to $75,000 of equity plus a $400 wildcard exemption. Federal exemption: You may exempt up to $15,000 of equity plus an $800 wildcard exemption.
Virginia	You may exempt up to $5,000 of equity ($10,000 if a husband and wife file jointly), plus $500 per dependent; you may also add a $2,000 wildcard exemption if you are a disabled veteran.
Washington or Federal Exemption	Washington: You may exempt up to $30,000 of equity. Federal exemption: You may exempt up to $15,000 of equity plus an $800 wildcard exemption.
West Virginia	You may exempt up to $15,000 of equity plus a $800 wildcard exemption.
Wisconsin or Federal Exemption	Wisconsin: You may exempt up to $40,000 of equity. Federal exemption: You may exempt up to $15,000 of equity plus an $800 wildcard exemption.
Wyoming	You may exempt up to $10,000 of equity ($20,000 if a husband and wife file jointly). If you live in a mobile home, you may exempt up to $6,000 of equity ($12,000 if a husband and wife file jointly).

c. Keeping Your House When You Have Nonexempt Equity

If you have nonexempt equity in your home and would lose it if you filed for Chapter 7 bankruptcy, you probably want to explore other options.

Reduce your equity. If you can reduce your equity, you may be able to pay off your other debts and avoid bankruptcy altogether. If you still need to file for bankruptcy after reducing your equity, you may be able to save your house. There are two ways to reduce your equity:.

- *Borrow against the equity.* One way to do this is to refinance your mortgage for more than you currently owe.

Example: You owe $180,000 on your mortgage at 9%. You have 22 years left on your mortgage, and your monthly payments are $1,568. Your house is worth $240,000, giving you $60,000 of equity, more than your state's homestead exemption of $30,000. You also owe $35,000 to the IRS, among other debts. You refinance your mortgage, reducing your interest rate to 7% and borrowing $215,000 ($180,000 to pay off your mortgage and $35,000 to pay off the IRS). You take out a 30-year loan and reduce your monthly payments to $1,430. In addition, your equity is now $25,000 ($240,000 - $215,000), within the homestead exemption.

Another way to borrow against the equity is to take out a home equity loan or line of credit. You may be able to pay off some high-interest debts, such as credit card bills, and avoid bankruptcy. Or you can pay off debts you wouldn't be able to discharge, such as support, taxes or a recent student loan, and still file for bankruptcy on the other debts.

- *Sell part ownership of your house.* By owning your home jointly with someone else, your equity is reduced by the percentage owned by the other person.

REDUCING YOUR EQUITY: TIMING IS KEY

If you decide to take steps to reduce the equity in your house, timing is key. Most likely, you will have to wait at least 90 days after refinancing or making payments on an equity line of credit before you file your bankruptcy case. That is because all payments you make during the 90 days before you file for bankruptcy can be set aside unless they were made in the normal course of business, such as making your regular mortgage payment, paying your utility bills, buying food and the like. Payments made to a friend, relative or close business associate up to one year before you file for bankruptcy can also be set aside, unless they were made in the normal course of business. So if you decide to reduce your equity by selling part ownership of your house to someone else, you'll most likely have to wait three months to a year before filing.

Offer to substitute cash for the amount of nonexempt equity. If you want to file for Chapter 7 bankruptcy, but you're afraid you will lose your house because your equity exceeds the homestead amount, you might be able to save your house if you have cash on hand you can give the trustee instead. You may be able to raise the cash by selling exempt property or using income you earn after you file.

File for Chapter 13 bankruptcy. Chapter 13 bankruptcy lets you pay your debts out of your income, rather than by selling your property. Thus, if you file for Chapter 13 bankruptcy, you won't give up your home even if you have nonexempt equity.

2. If You're Behind on Your Mortgage Payments

If you're behind on your house payments and looking for a solution, you have a number of options available to you, although Chapter 7 bankruptcy probably isn't one of them. The automatic stay won't permanently prevent foreclosure—the right of a mortgage lender to sell your house at a public auction and keep the proceeds. At most, it will slow down the foreclosure proceedings for a month or so. About the only way Chapter 7 bankruptcy can help you is if you can stave off foreclosure for the length of your bankruptcy case—when it's over, you should have an easier time making your mortgage payments.

a. Negotiating With the Lender

If you've missed only a few mortgage payments, most lenders are willing to negotiate. What the lender agrees to will depend on your credit history, the reason for your missed payments and your financial prospects.

Here are the possible options your lender might agree to:

- Spread out the repayment of the missed payments over a few months.
- Reduce or suspend your regular payments for a specified time and then add a portion of your overdue amount to your regular payments later on.
- Extend the length of your loan and add the missed payments at the end.
- Suspend the principal portion of your monthly payment for a while and have you pay only interest, taxes and insurance.
- Refinance your loan to reduce future monthly payments.

b. If the Lender Starts to Foreclose

If your debt problems look severe or long-lasting, the lender may take steps toward foreclosure. In most cases, before foreclosure actually occurs the lender will accelerate the loan. This means you must pay the entire balance immediately. If you don't, the lender is entitled to foreclose.

There are two different kinds of foreclosure. One is called a judicial foreclosure because the lender must file papers in court and obtain the court's approval before foreclosing. This kind of foreclosure can take as long as 18-36 months before you would ever lose your house. If you file for Chapter 7 bankruptcy, your bankruptcy will have little effect on this type of foreclosure. Your bankruptcy will probably start and end before much happens in the foreclosure case. Remember, Chapter 7 bankruptcy takes only four to six months. The only real effect is that your lender will be barred from sending you foreclosure notices or proceeding with a court hearing unless it files a motion with the court to have the automatic stay lifted. And even if the stay is lifted, it won't effect your bankruptcy.

The other kind of foreclosure is called a nonjudicial foreclosure because the lender does not have to go to court in order to foreclose. Instead, a third-party trustee sells your property after sending you a series of notices. The trustee is the person or business named in a deed of trust which you signed instead of, or in addition to, a traditional mortgage when you purchased or refinanced your property. Nonjudicial foreclosures can happen quickly, sometimes in as few as four months, the same amount of time you are likely to be in a Chapter 7 bankruptcy case. If you do file, expect the mortgage lender to come to court and request that the automatic stay be lifted. If you have nonexempt equity in your home, the bankruptcy trustee is likely to successfully oppose the motion and sell the property herself so your unsecured creditors get that equity. If you have no equity, however, the trustee will probably grant the motion to lift the stay and let the foreclosure go through.

During a foreclosure, you have several options, although if the creditor begins a nonjudicial foreclosure, you may be cut off from some of them simply because of time constraints.

- **Sell your house.** If you don't get any offers that will cover what you owe your lender, the lender may agree to take less—called a short sale.

- **Get a new loan** that pays off all or part of the first loan and puts you on a new schedule of monthly payments. If the original lender has accelerated the loan, you'll need to refinance the entire balance of the loan to prevent foreclosure.

- **Reinstate the loan.** If the lender hasn't accelerated the loan, you can prevent foreclosure simply by paying the missed payments, taxes and insurance, plus interest.

- **File for Chapter 13 bankruptcy.** If your lender has started to foreclose, in a Chapter 13 bankruptcy you can make up your missed payments, reinstate the loan and keep making the payments under the original contract. This is called "curing the default." Your right to cure the default depends on how far along the foreclosure proceeding is. If the lender has accelerated the loan or obtained a foreclosure judgment, you usually can still cure the default. If the foreclosure sale has already occurred, you cannot cure the default through Chapter 13 bankruptcy. This is true even if your state law gives you a "redemption right," which lets you buy back the house from the person who bought it at the foreclosure sale as long as a new deed hasn't yet been recorded.

  You might also use Chapter 13 bankruptcy to buy time. For example, if your lender has begun foreclosure proceedings, you can file for Chapter 13 bankruptcy to put the automatic stay in place to stop collection efforts. During the time it takes for the lender to file a motion to have the stay lifted, for the court to schedule it and for you to appear to argue it, you may be able to sell the house. You can then dismiss your case, unless, however, you have other debts you want to take care of through a Chapter 13 case.

c. If Foreclosure Is Unavoidable

If it looks like foreclosure is inevitable, losing your home in bankruptcy is often better than losing it in a foreclosure sale.

A forced sale of your home in bankruptcy is supervised by the bankruptcy trustee, who will want to sell the house for as much as possible. (Remember, the job of the trustee is to generate as much money as possible for your unsecured creditors.) If you have some equity in the house that you'd be entitled to under a homestead exemption, the more the house sells for, the more likely it is that you will get some or all of the exemption. In a foreclosure sale, on the other hand, the foreclosing creditor will try to get only a price high enough to cover the amount due on the mortgage. You're more than likely going to lose any equity you have in the house.

B. Renting and Filing for Bankruptcy

If you are current on your rent payments and file for either Chapter 7 or Chapter 13 bankruptcy, it's highly unlikely your landlord would ever find out. You won't be listing your landlord as a creditor because you aren't behind. Although you have to list on your bankruptcy papers any security deposits held by your landlord, most debtors can claim such deposits as exempt. Even if you can't, it's a rare trustee who actually goes after that money.

About the only time your landlord would find out about your bankruptcy is if she goes through your mail (you'll be sent notices from the bankruptcy court) or enters your premises without your knowledge and sees your bankruptcy papers in plain view. In this situation, your landlord may very well be violating state rules on privacy, and you probably have more problems on your hands than just unmanageable debts.

If you are behind on your rent, there's a good chance that your landlord will begin eviction proceedings to get you out. Your inclination may be to file for bankruptcy—either Chapter 7 or Chapter 13—just to get the automatic stay in place to stop the eviction. This will work, but not for very long. Soon after you file, expect your landlord to come barreling into court to have the stay lifted. Filing for bankruptcy has become a favorite tactic for some eviction defense clinics, who file a bare-bones bankruptcy petition to stop evictions even if the tenant's debts don't justify bankruptcy. In response, many bankruptcy courts are willing to grant landlords immediate relief from the stay without looking too closely at the case. This is true even if you have a legitimate bankruptcy.

CALIFORNIA LANDLORDS MIGHT IGNORE THE AUTOMATIC STAY ALTOGETHER

A California law allows a landlord who has sued for eviction and has won a judgment for possession (but not a money judgment for back rent) to enforce the judgment—that is, to let the marshal or sheriff evict—even if you file for bankruptcy. This California law probably violates the federal bankruptcy law. Bankruptcy law is under the power of the federal legislative body—Congress—and states are generally unable to make laws pertaining to bankruptcy. Nevertheless, California landlords often ignore bankruptcies filed just to stop the sheriff from evicting—and courts are enforcing the law.

Now is the time to complete the Chapter 4 questions on the "Should I File For Bankruptcy?" checklist.

Can I Keep My Car and Other Vital Items of Property?

Chapter 4 covered what happens to your home if you file for bankruptcy. But a house or apartment may not be the only property you're worried about losing.

Most people who file for bankruptcy desperately want to hold onto something—often a car. In this chapter, we help you figure out what property you're at risk of losing if you file for bankruptcy. Take heart, however: rarely does a person lose property in a bankruptcy case.

A. Chapter 7 Bankruptcy vs. Chapter 13 Bankruptcy

If you read Chapter 1, you learned that for many people, the best feature of Chapter 13 bankruptcy is that they can arrange their affairs in order to repay their debts without giving up any property. (Some people *want* to lose property in a Chapter 13 bankruptcy—they propose funding some or all of their repayment plan through the sale of property, such as a home.) Other than the voluntary selling of property, only in a rare situation might you lose property in a Chapter 13 case. That usually involves missing payments on a secured debt and the bankruptcy court letting the creditor repossess or foreclose on the property securing the debt (the collateral).

Chapter 7 bankruptcy is different. If you own property that is considered nonexempt, you may lose it, its cash equivalent or other property of the same value to the bankruptcy trustee. In addition, if you aren't current on a secured debt or can't afford to make payments on it in the future, you may lose the property that secures the debt in a Chapter 7 case.

This chapter covers Chapter 7 bankruptcy cases only.

B. Exempt and Nonexempt Property

The property you own on the day you file for bankruptcy is called your bankruptcy estate. With a very few exceptions (discussed below), property you acquire after you file for bankruptcy isn't included in your bankruptcy estate. When you file for bankruptcy, on one of the forms you list all the property in your estate. On another form, you list the property you claim is exempt.

1. What's in Your Bankruptcy Estate

Several categories of property make up your bankruptcy estate.

Property you own and possess. Everything in your possession—for example, a car, real estate, clothing, books, TV, stereo system, furniture, tools, boat, artworks or stock certificates—is included in your bankruptcy estate. Property you have control of but which belongs to someone else is not part of your bankruptcy estate, because you don't have the right to sell it or give it away.

Property you own but don't possess. You can own something even if you don't have physical possession of it. For instance, you may own a car that someone else is using. Other examples include a deposit held by a stockbroker, a security deposit held by your landlord or a utility company or a business you've invested money in.

Property you are entitled to receive. Property that you have a legal right to receive but haven't yet when you file for bankruptcy is included in your bankruptcy estate. Common examples include:

- wages you have earned but have not yet been paid
- a tax refund legally due you
- vacation or termination pay you've earned
- property you've inherited but not yet received from someone who has died
- proceeds of an insurance policy, if the death, injury or other event that gives rise to payment has occurred, and
- money owed you for goods or services you've provided—accounts receivable.

Property you own with your spouse (if you are filing alone). If you're married but filing alone, your state's law determines which property is part of your bankruptcy estate and which isn't.

If you live in a community property state (Arizona, California, Idaho, Louisiana, Nevada, New Mexico, Texas, Washington or Wisconsin), as a general rule, all property either spouse acquires during the marriage is community property, owned jointly by both. Gifts and inheritances received specifically by one spouse are the common exceptions. If you're married and file for bankruptcy, all the community property you and your spouse own is considered part of your bankruptcy estate, even if your spouse doesn't file. If you file alone, your separate property (everything that isn't community) is also part of your bankruptcy estate. Your spouse's separate property isn't.

If you file for bankruptcy in a non-community property state (all states other than the nine listed above), your bankruptcy estate includes your separate property (property that has only your name on a title certificate or that was purchased, received as a gift or inherited by you alone), and half of the property jointly owned by you and your spouse.

Property you receive within 180 days after filing for bankruptcy. Most property you acquire or become entitled to after you file for bankruptcy isn't included in your bankruptcy estate. But there are a few exceptions. If you acquire or become entitled to the following items within 180 days after you file, you must amend your papers to include these items as part of your bankruptcy estate:

- property you inherit
- property from a marital settlement agreement or divorce decree, and
- death benefits or life insurance policy proceeds.

2. What's Exempt

To figure out what property is exempt, begin by making a list of what you own. If you need help compiling this list, take a look at the checklist of commonly owned property items, below. If you're married and filing jointly, enter all property owned by you and your spouse.

PERSONAL PROPERTY (SCHEDULE B)

Cash on hand (include sources)
☐ In your home
☐ In your wallet
☐ Under your mattress

Deposits of money (include sources)
☐ Bank account
☐ Brokerage account (with stockbroker)
☐ Certificates of deposit (CD)
☐ Credit union deposit
☐ Escrow account
☐ Money market account
☐ Money in a safe deposit box
☐ Savings and loan deposit

Security deposits
☐ Electric
☐ Gas
☐ Heating oil
☐ Security deposit on a rental unit
☐ Prepaid rent
☐ Rented furniture or equipment
☐ Telephone
☐ Water

Household goods, supplies and furnishings
☐ Antiques
☐ Appliances
☐ Carpentry tools
☐ China and crystal
☐ Clocks
☐ Dishes
☐ Food (total value)
☐ Furniture (list every item; go from room to room so you don't miss anything)
☐ Gardening tools
☐ Home computer (for personal use)
☐ Iron and ironing board
☐ Lamps
☐ Lawn mower or tractor
☐ Microwave oven
☐ Patio or outdoor furniture
☐ Radios
☐ Rugs
☐ Sewing machine
☐ Silverware and utensils
☐ Small appliances
☐ Snow blower
☐ Stereo system
☐ Telephone and answering machines

☐ Televisions
☐ Vacuum cleaner
☐ Video equipment (VCR, camcorder)

Books, pictures and other art objects; stamp, coin and other collections
☐ Art prints
☐ Bibles
☐ Books
☐ Coins
☐ Collectibles (such as political buttons, baseball cards)
☐ Family portraits
☐ Figurines
☐ Original art works
☐ Photographs
☐ Records, CDs, audiotapes
☐ Stamps
☐ Video tapes

Apparel
☐ Clothing
☐ Furs

Jewelry
☐ Engagement and wedding rings
☐ Gems
☐ Precious metals
☐ Watches

Firearms, sports equipment and other hobby equipment
☐ Board games
☐ Bicycle
☐ Camera equipment
☐ Electronic musical equipment
☐ Exercise machine
☐ Fishing gear
☐ Guns (rifles, pistols, shotguns, muskets)
☐ Model or remote cars or planes
☐ Musical instruments
☐ Scuba diving equipment
☐ Ski equipment
☐ Other sports equipment
☐ Other weapons (swords and knives)

Interests in insurance policies
☐ Credit insurance
☐ Disability insurance
☐ Health insurance
☐ Homeowner's or renter's insurance

☐ Term life insurance
☐ Whole life insurance

Annuities

Pension or profit-sharing plans

☐ IRA
☐ Keogh
☐ Pension or retirement plan
☐ 401(k) plan

Stock and interests in incorporated and unincorporated companies

Interests in partnerships

☐ Limited partnership interest
☐ General partnership interest

Government and corporate bonds and other investment instruments

☐ Corporate bonds
☐ Municipal bonds
☐ Promissory notes
☐ U.S. savings bonds

Accounts receivable

☐ Accounts receivable from business
☐ Commissions already earned

Family support

☐ Alimony (spousal support, maintenance) due under court order
☐ Child support payments due under court order
☐ Payments due under divorce property settlement

Other debts owed you where the amount owed is known and definite

☐ Disability benefits due
☐ Disability insurance due
☐ Judgments obtained against third parties you haven't yet collected
☐ Sick pay earned
☐ Social Security benefits due
☐ Tax refund due under returns already filed
☐ Vacation pay earned
☐ Wages due
☐ Worker's compensation due

Powers exercisable for your benefit, other than those listed under real estate

☐ Right to receive, at some future time, cash, stock or other personal property placed in an irrevocable trust
☐ Current payments of interest or principal from a trust

☐ General power of appointment over personal property

Interest due to another person's death

☐ Beneficiary of a living trust, if the trustor has died
☐ Expected proceeds from a life insurance policy where the insured has died
☐ Inheritance from an existing estate in probate (the owner has died and the court is overseeing the distribution of the property) even if the final amount is not yet known
☐ Inheritance under a will that is contingent upon one or more events occurring, but only if the owner has died

All other contingent claims and claims where the amount owed you is not known, including tax refunds, counterclaims and rights to setoff claims (claims you think you have against a person, government or corporation, but haven't yet sued on)

☐ Claims against a corporation, government entity or individual
☐ Potential tax refund but return not yet filed

Patents, copyrights and other intellectual property

☐ Copyrights
☐ Patents
☐ Trade secrets
☐ Trademarks
☐ Trade names

Licenses, franchises and other general intangibles

☐ Building permits
☐ Cooperative association holdings
☐ Exclusive licenses
☐ Liquor licenses
☐ Nonexclusive licenses
☐ Patent licenses
☐ Professional licenses

Automobiles and other vehicles

☐ Car
☐ Mini bike or motor scooter
☐ Mobile or motor home if on wheels
☐ Motorcycle
☐ Recreational vehicle (RV)
☐ Trailer
☐ Truck
☐ Van

Boats, motors and accessories

☐ Boat (canoe, kayak, rowboat, shell, sailboat, pontoon, yacht, etc.)
☐ Boat radar, radio or telephone

☐ Outboard motor

Aircraft and accessories

☐ Aircraft
☐ Aircraft radar, radio and other accessories

Office equipment, furnishings and supplies

☐ Artwork in your office
☐ Computers, software, modems, printers
☐ Copier
☐ Fax machine
☐ Furniture
☐ Rugs
☐ Supplies
☐ Telephones
☐ Typewriters

Machinery, fixtures, equipment and supplies used in business

☐ Military uniforms and accoutrements
☐ Tools of your trade

Business inventory

Livestock, poultry and other animals

☐ Birds
☐ Cats
☐ Dogs
☐ Fish and aquarium equipment
☐ Horses
☐ Other pets
☐ Livestock and poultry

Crops—growing or harvested

Farming equipment and implements

Farm supplies, chemicals and feed

Other personal property of any kind not already listed

☐ Church pew
☐ Health aids (for example, wheelchair, crutches)
☐ Hot tub or portable spa
☐ Season tickets

Value of your property. After listing your property, enter a value for each item. It's easy to enter a dollar amount for your cash and most investments. If you own a car, start with the low *Kelley Blue Book* price. If the car needs repair, reduce the value by the amount it would cost you to fix the car. You can find the *Kelley Blue Book* at a public library or online at http://www.kbb.com. For most other property, estimate what you could sell it for at a garage sale or through a classified ad. As long as your estimates are reasonable, the lower the value you place on property, the more of it you will probably be allowed to keep through the bankruptcy process.

If you own an item of property jointly with someone other than a spouse with whom you would file for bankruptcy, reduce the value of the item to reflect only what you own. For example, you and your brother jointly bought a music synthesizer worth $10,000. Your ownership share is 40% and your brother's is 60%. You'd list the value of the property at $4,000, not $10,000.

Equity in your property. If the property is collateral for a secured debt—either the loan taken out to purchase the item or a separate loan for which you pledged the property as collateral—write down the amount of the secured claims next to the value of the property. Continuing with the above example, if you and your brother financed the purchase of the synthesizer and gave the seller the right to repossess it if you default, the amount you still owe is the secured claim.

Your equity is the amount you would get to keep if you sold the property. It's the value of the property minus the amount of any secured claims. Equity is an important concept in determining if your property is exempt.

Example: You bought a new car two years ago. You made a $3,000 down payment and financed the rest, $15,000 over five years at 6%, with the dealer. The car's value is now $11,500, and you still owe $9,500. Your equity is $2,000 ($11,500 - $9,500).

a. An Overview of Exemptions

The federal Bankruptcy Code provides a list of exemptions. The Code also allows states to "opt out" of the federal exemptions and, instead, to require its debtors to use the exemptions offered under state law. If a state has not opted out, the debtors in that state can use either their state's exemptions or the federal exemptions.

Under both the federal and state exemption systems, some types of property are exempt regardless of value. Other kinds of property are exempt up to a limit. For instance, cars are often exempt up to a certain amount—usually between $1,200 and $2,500. An exemption limit means that any equity above the limit is considered nonexempt. The trustee can take the property and sell it, give you the exemption amount (theoretically so you can replace the item that is sold) and distribute the remainder to your creditors.

b. Determining Which of Your Property Is Exempt

Very few people lose property in Chapter 7 bankruptcy. Only if you have the kind of property listed below—and you don't want to lose it—should you be concerned:

- substantial equity in a motor vehicle
- expensive musical instruments
- stamp, coin and other collections
- cash, deposit accounts, stocks, bonds and other investments
- business assets
- valuable artwork
- expensive clothing and jewelry, or
- family heirlooms.

To figure out what property is exempt in your state, take a look at the chart below.

The chart below provides the exemptions for only certain categories of property. A complete list of exempt property can be found in *How to File for Chapter 7 Bankruptcy*, by Stephen Elias, Albin Renauer and Robin Leonard or *Chapter 13 Bankruptcy: Repay Your Debts*, by Robin Leonard (both published by Nolo).

PENSIONS AND RETIREMENT PLANS

If you own a pension that is covered by the federal law ERISA (Employee Retirement Income Security Act), it is not considered part of your bankruptcy estate, and so you are at no risk of losing it. The reason is somewhat complex, involving both ERISA law and bankruptcy law. Essentially, the pension is not considered property of the estate because you have limited access to the money.

To find out whether or not your pension is covered by ERISA, call the benefits coordinator on your job or the pension plan administrator.

In most states, non-ERISA retirement benefits are exempt. You could be at risk of losing an IRA, however. Check with a knowledgeable bankruptcy attorney in your area if you are concerned about losing any retirement benefits.

PROPERTY EXEMPT IN BANKRUPTCY

State	Motor vehicles	Miscellaneous personal property	Tools of your trade	Wildcard exemption
Alabama	None.	Books, necessary clothing, family portraits and pictures.	None.	$3,000 of any property.
Alaska	$3,450 of equity, as long as the market value does not exceed $23,000.	$3,450 of books, musical instruments, clothing, family portraits, household goods and heirlooms; $1,500 of jewelry.	$3,220 of implements, books and tools.	None.
Arizona	$1,500 of equity. $4,000 of equity if you are disabled.	$4,000 of 2 beds and living room chair per person; 1 dresser, property table, lamp, bedding per bed; kitchen table; dining room table and 4 chairs; living room carpet or rug; couch; 3 lamps; 3 coffee or end tables; pictures, paintings, drawings done by debtor; family portraits; refrigerator; stove; TV, radio or stereo; alarm clock; washer; dryer; vacuum cleaner to total. $150 in one bank account. $500 from a Bible, bicycle, sewing machine, typewriter, rifle, pistol or shotgun. $250 of books; $500 of clothing; $1,000 wedding and engagement rings; $100 watch; $250 of musical instruments.	$2,500 of implements, books and tools. $2,500 of farm machinery, utensils, seed, instruments of husbandry, feed, grain and animals. Teaching aids of a teacher.	None.
Arkansas or Federal Exemptions	$1,200 of equity (Arkansas). $2,400 of equity (Federal Exemptions).	Clothing; wedding bands—diamond cannot exceed 1/2 carat (Arkansas). $8,075 of animals, crops, clothing, appliances, books, furnishings, household goods, musical instruments (maximum $425 per item); $1,075 of jewelry (Federal Exemptions).	$750 of implements, books and tools (Arkansas). $1,500 of implements, books and tools (Federal Exemptions).	$500 of any property for head of family, $200 otherwise (Arkansas). $800 of any property, plus another $7,500 if you don't claim a homestead (Federal Exemptions).
California System 1 or System 2	$1,900 of equity or $5,000 of equity if vehicle needed for work, other than commuting (System 1). $2,400 of equity (System 2).	Appliances, furnishings, clothing needed and $5,000 of jewelry, heirlooms and art (System 1). Animals, crops, appliances, furnishings, household goods, books, musical instruments and clothing to $400 per item, and $1,000 of jewelry (System 2).	$5,000 ($10,000 if spouses in same occupation) of implements, books and tools (System 1). $1,500 of implements, books and tools (System 2).	None (System 1). $800 of any property, plus another $15,000 if you don't claim a homestead (System 2).

State	Motor vehicles	Miscellaneous personal property	Tools of your trade	Wildcad Exemption
Colorado	$1,000 of equity. $3,000 of equity if you are elderly or disabled and need the vehicle to get medical care.	$750 of clothing, $1,500 of household goods, $500 of jewelry and articles of adornment and $750 of pictures and books.	$1,500 of books of professional or $1,500 of implements, books and tools of others. $2,000 of farm tools and $3,000 of farm animals.	None.
Connecticut or Federal Exemptions	$1,500 of equity (Connecticut). $2,400 of equity (Federal Exemptions).	Appliances, clothing, furniture and bedding needed; wedding and engagement rings (Connecticut). $8,075 of animals, crops, clothing, appliances, books, furnishings, household goods, musical instruments (maximum $425 per item); $1,075 of jewelry (Federal Exemptions).	Necessary implements, books, tools and farm animals (Connecticut). $1,500 of implements, books and tools (Federal Exemptions).	$1,000 of any property (Connecticut). $800 of any property, plus another $7,500 if you don't claim a homestead (Federal Exemptions).
Delaware	None.	Bible, books, family pictures, clothing, jewelry, pianos, leased organs and sewing machines.	$75 of implements, books and tools (New Castle and Sussex Counties); $50 of implements, books and tools (Kent County).	$500 of any property
District of Columbia or Federal Exemptions	None (District of Columbia). $2,400 of equity (Federal Exemptions).	$300 of beds, bedding, radios, cooking utensils, stoves, furniture, furnishings and sewing machines; $400 of books; $300 of clothing; family pictures (District of Columbia). $8,075 of animals, crops, clothing, appliances, books, furnishings, household goods, musical instruments (maximum $425 per item); $1,075 of jewelry (Federal Exemptions).	$300 of furniture, implements, books and tools of professional or artist. $200 of implements, books and tools of mechanic (District of Columbia). $1,500 of implements, books and tools (Federal Exemptions).	None (District of Columbia). $800 of any property, plus another $7,500 if you don't claim a homestead (Federal Exemptions).
Florida	$1,000 of equity.	$1,000 of any personal property.	None.	None.
Georgia	$1,000 of equity.	$3,500 of animals, crops, clothing, appliances, books, furnishings, household goods, musical instruments (maximum $400 per item); $500 of jewelry.	$500 of implements, books and tools.	$400 of any property, plus another $5,000 if you don't claim a homestead.

State	Motor vehicles	Miscellaneous personal property	Tools of your trade	Wildcad Exemption
Hawaii or Federal Exemptions	$1,000 wholesale value or unlimited value if vehicle needed for work, other than commuting (Hawaii). $2,400 of equity (Federal Exemptions).	Appliances and furnishings needed; books, clothing, $1,000 of jewelry and articles of adornment (Hawaii). $8,075 of animals, crops, clothing, appliances, books, furnishings, household goods, musical instruments (maximum $425 per item); $1,075 of jewelry (Federal Exemptions).	Necessary implements, books and tools (Hawaii). $1,500 of implements, books and tools (Federal Exemptions).	None (Hawaii). $800 of any property, plus another $7,500 if you don't claim a homestead (Federal Exemptions).
Idaho	$3,000 of equity.	$4,000 of appliances, furnishings, books, clothing, pets, musical instruments, 1 firearm, family portraits and sentimental heirlooms (maximum $500 per item); $250 of jewelry.	$1,500 of implements, books and tools.	None.
Illinois	$1,200 of equity.	Bible, family pictures, schoolbooks and needed clothing.	$750 of implements, books and tools.	$2,000 of any property
Indiana	None.	None.	None.	$4,000 of any tangible property; $100 of any intangible property.
Iowa	$5,000 of equity.	$2,000 of appliances, furnishings and household goods; $1,000 of bibles, books, portraits, pictures and paintings; $1,000 of clothing plus receptacles to hold clothing; $1,000 tax refund; musical instruments (motor vehicle, tax refund and musical instruments cannot exceed $5,000 total) rifle or musket; shotgun; wedding or engagement rings.	$10,000 of either farming or nonfarming equipment.	$100 of any personal property.
Kansas	$20,000 of equity. If equipped for a disabled person, unlimited.	Clothing, furnishings and household equipment, $1,000 of jewelry and articles of adornment.	$7,500 of implements, books and tools.	None.
Kentucky	$2,500 of equity.	$3,000 of clothing, jewelry, articles of adornment and furnishings.	$1,000 of implements, books and tools and $2,500 of equity in a vehicle of professional. $3,000 of implements and tools of farmer. $300 of implements, books and tools of nonfarmer.	$1,000 of any property.

State	Motor vehicles	Miscellaneous personal property	Tools of your trade	Wildcad Exemption
Louisiana	Pickup truck (maximum 3 tons) or non-luxury auto and utility trailer if vehicle need for work, other than commuting.	Arms, military accouterments, bedding, linens, bedroom furniture, chinaware, glassware, utensils, silverware (non-sterling), clothing, family portraits, musical instruments, heating and cooling equipment, living room and dining room furniture, pressing irons, sewing machine, refrigerator, freezer, stove, washer and dryer; $5,000 of engagement and wedding rings.	Necessary implements, books and tools, including a vehicle (other than to commute).	None.
Maine	$2,500 of equity.	Animals, crops, musical instruments, books, clothing, furnishings, household goods and appliances (maximum $200 per item); cooking stove, furnaces, stoves for heat; $750 of jewelry (no limit for 1 wedding and 1 engagement ring).	$5,000 of implements, books and tools. Boat (up to five tons) of commercial fisherman. One of each type of necessary farm implement.	$400 of any property, plus another $6,000 if you don't claim a homestead.
Maryland	None.	$500 of appliances, furnishings, household goods, books, pets and clothing.	$2,500 of implements, books and tools.	$5,500 of any property.
Massachusetts or Federal Exemptions	$700 of equity (Massachusetts). $2,400 of equity (Federal Exemptions).	Beds, bedding and heating unit; clothing needed; $200 of bibles and books; $200 sewing machine; 2 cows, 12 sheep, 2 swine, 4 tons of hay; $3,000 of furniture (Massachusetts). $8,075 of animals, crops, clothing, appliances, books, furnishings, household goods, musical instruments (maximum $425 per item); $1,075 of jewelry (Federal Exemptions).	$500 of implements, books and tools. $500 of boats, tackle and nets of fisherman. $500 of material you designed (Massachusetts). $1,500 of implements, books and tools (Federal Exemptions).	None (Massachusetts). $800 of any property, plus another $7,500 if you don't claim a homestead (Federal Exemptions).
Michigan	$1,000 of equity if vehicle needed for work, other than commuting.	$1,000 of appliances, utensils, books, furniture and household goods; clothing, family pictures, 2 cows, 100 hens, 5 roosters, 10 sheep, 5 swine; hay and grain.	$1,000 of implements, books and tools.	None.

State	Motor vehicles	Miscellaneous personal property	Tools of your trade	Wildcad Exemption
Minnesota or Federal Exemptions	$3,400 of equity. If modified for a disabled person, $34,000 of equity (Minnesota). $2,400 of equity (Federal Exemptions).	$7,650 of appliances, furniture, radio, phonographs and TV; bible, books and musical instruments; clothing (includes watch) and utensils (Minnesota). $8,075 of animals, crops, clothing, appliances, books, furnishings, household goods, musical instruments (maximum $425 per item); $1,075 of jewelry (Federal Exemptions).	$13,000 of farming equipment. $8,000 of implements, books and tools. Teaching materials of public school teacher (Minnesota). $1,500 of implements, books and tools (Federal Exemptions).	None (Minnesota). $7,500 if you don't claim a homestead (Federal Exemptions).
Mississippi	None.	None.	None.	$10,000 of any tangible personal property.
Missouri	$1,000 of equity.	$1,000 of appliances, household goods, furnishings, clothing, books, crops, animals and musical instruments; $500 of jewelry.	$2,000 of implements, books and tools.	$1,250 (plus $250 per child) of any property if head of family, $400 otherwise.
Montana	$1,200 of equity.	$4,500 of appliances, household furnishings, goods, crops, musical instruments, books, firearms, sporting goods, clothing and jewelry (maximum $600 per item).	$3,000 of implements books and tools.	None.
Nebraska	$2,400 of equity if vehicle needed for work, including commuting.	Clothing needed; $1,500 of furniture and kitchen utensils.	$2,400 of implements, books and tools.	$2,500 of any personal property if you don't claim a homestead.
Nevada	$4,500 of equity. If equipped for a disabled person, unlimited.	$3,000 of appliances, household goods, furniture, home and yard equipment; $1,500 of books; keepsakes and pictures; metal-bearing ores, geological specimens, art curiosities or paleontological remains; 1 gun.	$4,500 of dwelling, implements and tools of miner. $4,500 of farming equipment. $4,500 of implements, books and tools.	None.

State	Motor vehicles	Miscellaneous personal property	Tools of your trade	Wildcad Exemption
New Hampshire or Federal Exemptions	$4,000 of equity (New Hampshire). $2,400 of equity (Federal Exemptions).	Clothing, beds, bedsteads, bedding and cooking utensils needed; $800 of bibles and books; cooking and heating stoves, refrigerator; cow, 6 sheep, 4 tons of hay; $3,500 of furniture; $500 of jewelry; sewing machine (New Hampshire). $8,075 of animals, crops, clothing, appliances, books, furnishings, household goods, musical instruments (maximum $425 per item); $1,075 of jewelry (Federal Exemptions).	$5,000 of implements, books and tools (New Hampshire). $1,500 of implements, books and tools (Federal Exemptions).	$1,000 of any property (New Hampshire). $800 of any property, plus another $7,500 if you don't claim a homestead (Federal Exemptions).
New Jersey or Federal Exemptions	None (New Jersey). $2,400 of equity (Federal Exemptions).	$1,000 of furniture and household goods (New Jersey). $8,075 of animals, crops, clothing, appliances, books, furnishings, household goods, musical instruments (maximum $425 per item); $1,075 of jewelry (Federal Exemptions).	None (New Jersey). $1,500 of implements, books and tools (Federal Exemptions).	$1,000 of any personal property (New Jersey). $800 of any property, plus another $7,500 if you don't claim a homestead (Federal Exemptions).
New Mexico or Federal Exemptions	$4,000 of equity (New Mexico). $2,400 of equity (Federal Exemptions).	Books, furniture, clothing; $2,500 of jewelry (New Mexico). $8,075 of animals, crops, clothing, appliances, books, furnishings, household goods, musical instruments (maximum $425 per item); $1,075 of jewelry (Federal Exemptions).	$1,500 of implements, books and tools (New Mexico). $1,500 of implements, books and tools (Federal Exemptions).	$500 of any personal property, plus another $2,000 if you don't claim a homestead (New Mexico). $800 of any property, plus another $7,500 if you don't claim a homestead (Federal Exemptions).
New York	$2,400 of equity.	$5,000 of bible, schoolbooks, $50 of books, pictures, clothing, stoves, sewing machine, furniture, refrigerator, TV; radio, wedding ring, $35 watch, crockery, cooking utensils, tableware; $2,500 of cash if you don't claim a homestead.	$600 of implements, books and tools.	None.

State	Motor vehicles	Miscellaneous personal property	Tools of your trade	Wildcad Exemption
North Carolina	$1,500 of equity.	$3,500 (plus $750 per dependent, up to $3,000) of animals, crops, musical instruments, books, clothing, appliances, household goods and furnishings.	$750 of implements, books and tools.	$500 of any property, plus another $3,500 if you don't claim a homestead.
North Dakota	$1,200 of equity.	Bible, pictures, clothing, $100 of books and $7,500 of cash if you don't claim a homestead. In addition, head of household may exempt $1,500 of books and musical instruments; $1,000 of furniture, including bedsteads and bedding; $1,000 of tools used in profession; $4,500 of livestock and farm implements; and $1,000 of tools of mechanic and stock in trade.	None.	$5,000 of any personal property if you are head of household and don't claim the personal property exemptions to the left; $2,500 of any property if you are not head of household.
Ohio	$1,000 of equity.	$1,500 ($2,000 if you don't claim a homestead) of animals, crops, books, musical instruments, appliances, jewelry, household goods, furnishings, hunting and fishing equipment and firearms (maximum $200 per item); beds, bedding and clothing (maximum $200 per item); $400 of cash; $300 cooking unit, $300 refrigerator.	$750 of implements, books and tools.	$400 of any property.
Oklahoma	$3,000 of equity.	Books, portraits, pictures, 1 gun, 2 bridles, 2 saddles, 100 chickens, 10 hogs, 2 horses, 5 cows, 20 sheep, $4,000 of clothing and furniture.	$5,000 of implements, books and tools.	None.
Oregon	$1,700 of equity.	$7,500 of bank deposits; $600 of books, pictures and musical instruments; $1,800 of clothing, jewelry and other personal items; $3,000 of furniture, household items, utensils, radios and TVs; $1,000 of firearms.	$3,000 of implements, books and tools.	None.
Pennsylvania or Federal Exemptions	None (Pennsylvania). $2,400 of equity (Federal Exemptions).	Bibles, schoolbooks, sewing machine and clothing (Pennsylvania). $8,075 of animals, crops, clothing, appliances, books, furnishings, household goods, musical instruments (maximum $425 per item); $1,075 of jewelry (Federal Exemptions).	None (Pennsylvania). $1,500 of implements, books and tools (Federal Exemptions).	$300 of any property (Pennsylvania). $800 of any property, plus another $7,500 if you don't claim a homestead (Federal Exemptions).

State	Motor vehicles	Miscellaneous personal property	Tools of your trade	Wildcad Exemption
Rhode Island or Federal Exemptions	None (Rhode Island). $2,400 of equity (Federal Exemptions).	$1,000 of beds, bedding, furniture; $300 of bibles and books; clothing (Rhode Island). $8,075 of animals, crops, clothing, appliances, books, furnishings, household goods, musical instruments (maximum $425 per item); $1,075 of jewelry (Federal Exemptions).	$500 of working tools. Library of professional (Rhode Island). $1,500 of implements, books and tools (Federal Exemptions).	None (Rhode Island). $800 of any property, plus another $7,500 if you don't claim a homestead (Federal Exemptions).
South Carolina	$1,200 of equity.	$2,500 of animals, appliances, books, clothing, household goods, furnishings and musical instruments; $1,000 of cash if you don't claim a homestead; $500 of jewelry.	$750 of implements, books and tools.	None.
South Dakota	None.	Bible, pictures, clothing and $200 of books. In addition, head of household may exempt $200 of books and musical instruments, 2 cows, 5 swine, 25 sheep; $1,250 of farming machinery; $200 of furniture, including bedsteads and bedding.	$300 of tools used in profession. $200 of tools of mechanic and stock in trade.	$4,000 of any personal property if you are head of household and don't claim the personal property exemptions to the left; $2,000 of any property if you are not head of household.
Tennessee	None.	Bible, schoolbooks, pictures, portraits, clothing and their storage containers.	$1,900 of implements, books and tools.	$4,000 of any personal property.
Texas or Federal Exemptions	See next column (Texas). $2,400 of equity (Federal Exemptions).	$30,000 ($60,000 for head of family) of athletic and sporting equipment; 2 firearms; home furnishings, including family heirlooms; clothing; jewelry (not to exceed 25% of total exemption); 1 motor vehicle per member of family; 2 horses, mules or donkeys and a saddle, blanket and bridle for each; 12 head of cattle; 60 head of other types of livestock; 120 fowl (Texas). $8,075 of animals, crops, clothing, appliances, books, furnishings, household goods, musical instruments (maximum $425 per item); $1,075 of jewelry (Federal Exemptions).	Necessary implements, books and tools (Texas). $1,500 of implements, books and tools (Federal Exemptions).	None (Texas). $800 of any property, plus another $7,500 if you don't claim a homestead (Federal Exemptions).

State	Motor vehicles	Miscellaneous personal property	Tools of your trade	Wildcad Exemption
Utah	$2,500 of equity.	$500 of animals, books and musical instruments; artwork depicting, or done by, family member; bed, bedding, carpets, washer and dryer; clothing (cannot claim furs or jewelry); $500 of dining and kitchen tables and chairs; $500 of heirlooms; refrigerator, freezer, microwave, stove and sewing machine; $500 of sofas, chairs and related furnishings.	$3,500 of implements, books and tools. $2,500 of equity in a motor vehicle.	None.
Vermont or Federal Exemptions	$2,500 of equity (Vermont). $2,400 of equity (Federal Exemptions).	$2,500 of appliances, furnishings, goods, clothing, books, crops, musical instruments; 1 cow, 2 goats, 10 sheep, 10 chickens; 3 swarms of bees; 2 harnesses, 2 halters, 2 chains, plow and ox yoke; $500 of jewelry; wedding ring; stove, heating unit, refrigerator, freezer, water heater and sewing machines (Vermont). $8,075 of animals, crops, clothing, appliances, books, furnishings, household goods, musical instruments (maximum $425 per item); $1,075 of jewelry (Federal Exemptions).	$5,000 of implements, books and tools (Vermont). $1,500 of implements, books and tools (Federal Exemptions).	$400 of any property (Vermont). $800 of any property, plus another $7,500 if you don't claim a homestead (Federal Exemptions).
Virginia	$2,000 of equity.	Bible, wedding and engagement rings; $1,000 of clothing; $5,000 of family portraits and heirlooms; $5,000 of household furnishings.	$4,000 of farm equipment. $10,000 of implements, books and tools.	$5,000 of any personal property if you don't claim a homestead, plus another $2,000 of any property if you are a disabled veteran and a householder.
Washington or Federal Exemptions	$2,500 of equity (Washington). $2,400 of equity (Federal Exemptions).	$2,700 of appliances, furniture, household goods, home and yard equipment; $1,500 of books; clothing (no more than $1,000 of furs, jewelry, ornaments) keepsakes and pictures (Washington). $8,075 of animals, crops, clothing, appliances, books, furnishings, household goods, musical instruments (maximum $425 per item); $1,075 of jewelry (Federal Exemptions).	$5,000 of implements, books and tools (Washington). $1,500 of implements, books and tools (Federal Exemptions).	$1,000 of any personal property (Washington). $800 of any property, plus another $7,500 if you don't claim a homestead (Federal Exemptions).
West Virginia	$2,400 of equity.	$8,000 of animals, clothing, appliances, books, household goods, furnishings and musical instruments (maximum $400 per item) $1,000 of jewelry.	$1,500 of implements, books and tools	$800 of any property, plus another $15,000 if you don't claim a homestead.

State	Motor vehicles	Miscellaneous personal property	Tools of your trade	Wildcad Exemption
Wisconsin of Federal Exemptions	$1,200 of equity (Wisconsin). $2,400 of equity (Federal Exemptions).	$1,000 in deposit accounts; $5,000 of household goods and furnishings, clothing, keepsakes, jewelry, appliances, books, musical instruments, firearms, sporting goods, animals and other tangible property (Wisconsin). $8,075 of animals, crops, clothing, appliances, books, furnishings, household goods, musical instruments (maximum $425 per item); $1,075 of jewelry (Federal Exemptions).	$7,500 of implements, books and tools (Wisconsin). $1,500 of implements, books and tools (Federal Exemptions).	None (Wisconsin). $800 of any property, plus another $7,500 if you don't claim a homestead (Federal Exemptions).
Wyoming	$2,400 of equity.	$2,000 per person of bedding, furniture and household articles; bible, school-books and pictures; $1,000 of clothing and wedding rings.	$2,000 of implements, books and tools.	None.

If you own a lot of property which you are concerned you might lose in a Chapter 7 bankruptcy, you may still seriously consider Chapter 7 bankruptcy if any of the following are true:

- You are able to sell some nonexempt property before you file. You can use the proceeds to buy exempt property that will help you make a fresh financial start or to pay debts that won't be discharged by the bankruptcy. If you choose to pay some debts, you must delay filing for bankruptcy at least 90 days after making the payment, or one year if it was to a relative, close friend or business associate.

Be aware that your local bankruptcy court may consider these kinds of transfers an attempt to defraud your creditors. The only sure way to find out in advance what is and isn't permissible in your area is to ask people familiar with local bankruptcy court practices.

- Your debts are so high you're willing to give up some property in exchange for their discharge.
- You can raise enough cash to buy the nonexempt property you want back from the trustee.
- The property will be difficult or expensive for the trustee to sell and he is likely to abandon it (give it back to you). If it's an item of

property you've been having or would have trouble selling (such as an out-of-state unimproved lot), the trustee is likely to abandon it.

MOVING TO A STATE WITH MORE GENEROUS EXEMPTIONS

Some debtors take a look at the list of exemptions for their state and are horrified at how short the list is or how low the value of the items are. Their state isn't merely ungenerous—it seems downright cruel.

One couple tried to get around this problem by selling their assets, moving to Florida, buying a new house with the cash (Florida has an unlimited homestead exemption) and then filing for bankruptcy over a year after buying the house. The bankruptcy court, however, declared the purchase fraudulent and denied them the homestead exemption.

So be careful if you plan to move to improve your lot.

C. Property That Secures a Debt

Secured debts are debts linked to specific items of property (sometimes called collateral or security). The property guarantees payment of the debt; if the debt isn't paid, the creditor can take the property or force its sale to pay off the debt. Some secured debts you incur voluntarily—such as a mortgage or car loan. Others are imposed against your will—like tax liens and liens imposed on property to enforce a judgment.

Bankruptcy's effect on secured debts is different from that on other kinds of debts, because a secured debt consists of two parts:

- The first part is no different than an unsecured debt: it is personal liability for the debt, and it is what obligates you to pay the debt to the creditor. Bankruptcy wipes out your personal liability if the debt is dischargeable. Once your personal liability is eliminated, the creditor cannot sue you to collect the debt.

- The second part of a secured debt is the creditor's legal claim (lien or security interest) on the property that is collateral for the debt. A lien gives the creditor the right to repossess the property or force its sale if you do not pay the debt. During bankruptcy, you may be able to eliminate, or at least reduce, liens on secured property.

If you're behind on payments to a secured creditor, Chapter 7 bankruptcy probably won't help you. The creditor will ask the court to lift the automatic stay so that the creditor can begin or resume repossession proceedings. If you want to keep the property, you'll need to reinstate the loan outside of bankruptcy—that is, make up the missed payments and resume making your regular payments. If your lender has already accelerated the loan—declared the entire balance due—and won't let you reinstate it, you will have to file for Chapter 13. You can make up the missed payments in your plan as long as you make the regular payments called for under your original agreement.

If you are current on your payments on a secured debt and you file for Chapter 7 bankruptcy, you must let the bankruptcy court know whether you want to give up the property in exchange for wiping out the debt, or if you want to keep the property through one of the methods available in bankruptcy. This section describes how to give up or keep secured property in bankruptcy.

1. Surrender Property

Surrendering secured property simply means allowing the creditor to repossess or take the item or foreclose on the lien. It completely frees you from the debt—the lien is satisfied by your surrender of the property, and your personal liability is discharged by the bankruptcy.

The advantage of surrendering property is that it is a quick and easy way to completely rid yourself of a secured debt. The disadvantage, obviously, is that you lose the property.

2. Eliminate Liens in Bankruptcy

It may be possible during your bankruptcy case to eliminate or reduce a lien that attaches to an item of secured property. If you can eliminate, or "avoid," a lien, you get to keep the property free and clear without paying anything more to the creditor.

Lien avoidance has several important restrictions, however:

- You must be able to claim the property as exempt.

- The lien must be either a judicial lien or something called a nonpossessory nonpurchase money security interest, which is a lien you gave a creditor by pledging your existing property (such as your stereo system) to secure a new debt. A judicial lien or nonpossessory nonpurchase money security interest can be avoided only on the following exempt property:

  ✓ household furnishings, household goods, clothing, appliances, books, musical instruments or jewelry

  ✓ health aids professionally prescribed for you or a dependent

  ✓ the first $5,000 of a lien attaching to animals or crops held primarily for your personal, family or household use, or

  ✓ the first $5,000 of a lien attaching to tools used in your trade.

- You must have owned the property before the lien was "fixed" on it. This will always be the case with nonpossessory nonpurchase money security interests. It's usually the case with judicial liens, where you are sued, the person obtains a judgment and then records it against your property. If a lien (such as a promissory note for cash secured by an expensive motor vehicle) is recorded just before ownership title changes on the property, however, the lien would be fixed before you owned the property. This unusual situation is likely to arise only in divorce situations.

3. Redeem Property

You have the right to redeem property—buy it back from the creditor rather than have it taken by the creditor and sold to someone else. You pay the creditor the property's current market value, usually in a lump sum, and in return the lien is eliminated. You then own the property free and clear.

Redemption is a great option if you owe more than the property is worth. The creditor must accept the current value of the item as payment in full. The disadvantage is that, generally, redemption requires immediate lump-sum payment of the value of the item.

In addition, you have the right to redeem property only if all of the following are true:

- The debt is a consumer debt used for personal or household purposes. This means you cannot redeem property that secures business debts.
- The property is tangible personal property. Tangible property is property you can touch, such as a car or stereo system. Examples of intangible property include investments (stocks and bonds) or intellectual property rights (patents, trademarks and copyrights).
- The property is either claimed as exempt or abandoned by the trustee.

4. Reaffirm a Debt

When you reaffirm a debt, both the creditor's lien on the collateral and your personal liability survive bankruptcy intact—as if you never filed. You and the creditor draw up an agreement which sets out the amount you owe and the terms of the repayment. In return, you get to keep the property as long as you keep current on your payments.

Reaffirmation can be used when lien avoidance or redemption is unavailable or impractical. It provides a sure way to keep property, as long as you abide by the terms of the reaffirmation agreement. But because reaffirmation leaves you personally liable, there is no way to walk away from the debt, even if the property becomes worthless or you simply decide you no longer want it.

Because of the disadvantages of reaffirmation, it should be a last choice, not a first. Use it primarily to keep property you can't be without and only if you have good reason to believe you'll be able to pay off the balance still owed the creditor. Many people use reaffirmation to keep a car in bankruptcy.

5. Retain Property Without Reaffirming or Redeeming

Some bankruptcy courts will let you to keep secured property as long as you remain current on your payments under your contract with the creditor. If you fall behind, the creditor can take the property, but your personal liability for the debt is wiped out by the bankruptcy. This method is often referred to as "information reaffirmation" or "informal repayment." (Be aware that not all courts allow this method, but the trend is toward permitting it.)

Informal repayment can be used when lien avoidance or redemption is not available and allows for payments in installments rather than a lump sum. Unlike formal reaffirmation, informal repayment leaves you the option of walking away from a debt without being personally liable for the balance owed.

 Now is the time to complete the Chapter 5 questions on the "Should I File For Bankruptcy?" checklist.

Can I Keep My Credit Cards?

W hat will happen to your credit cards when you file for bankruptcy depends largely on the current status of your account, and to a lesser degree on who the creditor is. For this discussion, consider that your credit cards will fall into three possible categories:

- cards on which you have zero balance—that is, you're all paid up
- cards on which you have a balance but are current—that is, you make at least the minimum payment each month, and
- cards on which you are in default—that is, you haven't made any payments in a while.

A. Your Balance Is Zero

On your bankruptcy papers, you must list all people and business to whom you currently owe money. These are called your creditors. If you have a balance of zero on a credit card, you don't currently owe the issuer any money and you don't have to list it on your bankruptcy papers. This means you might come through bankruptcy—Chapter 7 or Chapter 13—still owning that credit card.

Notice that I did not say that you will definitely come through bankruptcy still owning that credit card. It's possible that the bankruptcy trustee will confiscate your credit cards, ask you about the creditors with whom you have a zero balance or demand that you write to them and tell them about your bankruptcy. This is more likely to happen in a Chapter 13 case, where the trustee must supervise your finances for three to five years, than in a Chapter 7 case, where the trustee won't care about debts you incur after filing.

It's also possible that a creditor will find out about your bankruptcy from some source other than you or the bankruptcy court—namely, a credit bureau. Sometimes, a credit bureau automatically sends a bankruptcy notice to creditors it has on file associated with a given consumer.

Example: You file for bankruptcy and include the following debts, among others: BigBank Visa, MediumBank MasterCard and LittleBank Visa. Your balance on your TinyBank MasterCard is $0, so you don't include that creditor on your bankruptcy papers. BigBank,

MediumBank and LittleBank each report to the credit bureaus that your accounts are in bankruptcy. The credit bureaus may search their databases for each account on file for you and send a bankruptcy notice to your creditors that have not reported your accounts in bankruptcy. This means that TinyBank will learn of your filing even though you didn't list it as a creditor on your bankruptcy papers.

Even if a creditor isn't sent a bankruptcy notice by a credit bureau, the creditor still may learn of your bankruptcy. Creditors with whom you do business are allowed to check the information on file about you at a credit bureau and often do, especially if they are considering increasing your credit limit or are worried that you may default on your account. A creditor that checks will see your bankruptcy and all other information in your report. The creditor may decide to terminate your credit, even though you don't owe that business a penny, on the ground that you are no longer a good credit risk. There is nothing you can do to stop this, short of begging that your account be reopened. You might emphasize that you can't file for Chapter 7 bankruptcy again for six years, meaning that you are quite a good risk. But if your pleas are ignored, don't get too worked up over it. There are other ways to get a credit card, if you really think you need one. (See Chapter 9.)

DON'T PAY OFF ONE CREDIT CARD WHILE IGNORING OTHERS JUST BEFORE YOU FILE

When you file for bankruptcy, you must indicate on your papers all of your recent financial transactions. The bankruptcy trustee is looking to see if you favored one creditor at the expense of others. Bankruptcy law calls payments made shortly before filing for bankruptcy (other than those made in the normal course of business, such as for rent or to the phone company) "preferences." Preferences are not allowed. The trustee can sue the creditor for the amount of the preference and take it back so that it can be distributed among all of your creditors.

In general, a preference exists when you pay $600 or more to a creditor within 90 days before filing for bankruptcy. (If you make payments to a creditor who is close to you—for example, a friend or relative—a preference is $600 or more paid within one year before filing. This wouldn't apply with a credit card issuer.) So the bottom line is this: if you want to keep a credit card by paying off the balance before filing, you must wait at least 91 days after your last payment before filing. And as the text above indicates, there is still no guarantee you will get to keep the card.

B.　You Owe Money But Are Current

If you owe money on a credit card, but have managed to eke out at least a minimum payment each month, you will have to list this creditor on your bankruptcy papers even though you aren't behind. Your bankruptcy—Chapter 7 or Chapter 13—may come as a great surprise to the creditor. In fact, credit card issuers have recently lamented the increase in "surprise" bankruptcies—cases filed by people not in default.

If you file a Chapter 7 bankruptcy and want to keep your credit card, you probably will be able to do so by offering to sign a reaffirmation agreement with the credit card issuer. In a reaffirmation agreement, you agree to repay the balance in full, as if you never filed for bankruptcy.

Before you do this, ask yourself why you would take such a step. For most people, the purpose of filing for bankruptcy is to get rid of debts, not to emerge still owing money. Admittedly, some people choose to file knowing that they won't be able to eliminate certain debts. But even in that situation, it almost never makes sense to come out of bankruptcy owing on a credit card you had before you filed—more likely, you will come out of bankruptcy still owing taxes or a student loan. If you want to have a credit card after bankruptcy, chances are very good that you'll be able to get one (see Chapter 9)—but one that starts with a zero balance, not with the amount you owed before you filed.

It's possible that when you file a Chapter 7 bankruptcy, the credit card issuer will ask you to sign a reaffirmation agreement even if you intend to wipe out the debt. The creditor may offer tempting terms—a reduction in the interest rate, a reduction of the balance you owe, an increase in your line of credit. But resist. To sign a reaffirmation agreement would probably defeat a major, if not the single, reason you filed—to get rid of your credit card debt.

If the creditor gets insistent or starts claiming that you incurred the credit card debt fraudulently, see Section D, below.

If you file for Chapter 13 bankruptcy, in your plan you will propose to repay your unsecured creditors, including your credit card issuers, some percentage of what you owe. (Remember that secured debts, unlike credit card debts, are generally repaid in full.) Chapter 13 plans are sometimes referred to by this percentage—for example, "the Moleens filed a 55% plan." In most cases, if you pay less than 100% of what you owe, the creditor will cancel your account. And remember that the trustee may confiscate your card anyway.

C. You Are in Default

What happens to a credit card when you are in default when you file for bankruptcy is fairly similar to what happens when you file when you are current but owe a balance, as discussed in Section C, just above. But there are two notable differences.

First, your creditors won't be surprised that you file. With more than one million people filing each year—discharging billions of dollars of credit card debt alone—bankruptcy filings are a frequent reality for credit card issuers. They may not like that truth, but it's the truth nonetheless.

This dislike highlights the second difference. If you file for bankruptcy when you are in default on a credit card, the creditor may aggressively take steps to keep you from discharging the debt. The creditor will first ask you to voluntarily sign a reaffirmation agreement. If you don't agree—and you shouldn't—the creditor might start playing hardball, as described in Section D, just below.

D. Creditors' Attempts to "Force" You to Keep Your Credit Card

There are two possible methods a credit card issuer may employ to try to force you to keep your credit card—and the balance on it. The issuer might:

- claim that the debt is not dischargeable, or
- claim that the debt is secured and that you must reaffirm it.

Note that this discussion applies in Chapter 7 bankruptcy only. In a Chapter 13 case, if the credit card issuer feels it is not receiving enough under your plan, it will raise its objections at the confirmation hearing. (See Chapter 1, Section D.2.b.)

1. Claims That the Debt Is Nondischargeable

Several types of debts can survive Chapter 7 bankruptcy. (See Chapter 3.) Most of these debts are automatically nondischargeable. Others, however, including debts incurred on the basis of fraud, survive bankruptcy only if the creditor successfully raises an objection in the bankruptcy court. A creditor wanting to raise such an objection must file something called a "Complaint to Determine Dischargeability of a Debt" as a part of your bankruptcy case. The filing of the complaint starts a regular lawsuit which proceeds as a part of your bankruptcy case. You would have to file a formal response to the complaint. If you don't, you could lose the case by default.

Increasingly, credit card issuers make the claim that debtors incur credit card debt fraudulently—although many raise it in a letter or at the meeting of the creditors, and never file a formal Complaint to Determine Dischargeability of a Debt. Bankruptcy law specifies two situations in which credit card fraud is presumed:

- you ran up debts of more than $1,075 for luxury goods or services within 60 days before filing for bankruptcy, or
- you took out cash advances totaling more than $1,075 within 60 days before you filed for bankruptcy.

In any other situation, there is no presumption of fraud, no matter what the credit card issuer claims. Still, this doesn't mean all other behavior is acceptable. If a credit card issuer pushes its claim and gets a case before the bankruptcy court, the court will look to the following factors to determine fraud:

- short time between incurring the charges and filing for bankruptcy
- incurring debt after consulting an attorney
- many charges under $50 to avoid pre-clearance of the charge by the credit card issuer when you've reached your credit limit
- charges after the card issuer has ordered you to return the card or sent past due notices
- changes in your pattern of use of the card
- charges after you're obviously insolvent—no job, income or savings
- charges for luxuries, and
- multiple charges on the same day.

Credit card recovery programs are quite aggressive. Visa brags that while only 30% of its members challenged any bankruptcies a few years ago, today 99% of its members do so. Visa and MasterCard employees typically review bankruptcy filings (as well as a customer's file with the bank that issued the credit) to discern the date of insolvency, and then challenge all charges made after that date. The banks claim that insolvency is evidenced by any of the following:

- A notation in the customer's file that the customer has met with an attorney.

- A rapid increase in spending, quickly followed by 60–90 days of quiet.
- The date noted on any attorney's fee statement, if the customer consults a lawyer for help with a bankruptcy.

Of course, because a creditor challenges your discharge of a credit card debt doesn't mean the creditor is right. In virtually every case, the creditor files a standard 15- to 20-paragraph Complaint to Determine Dischargeability of a Debt form that makes boldface conclusions with no supporting facts. The creditor rarely attaches statements for the account, but only a printout of the charges to which it is objecting.

Credit card issuers rarely win these cases when they go before a judge. Judges are finding that credit card issuers usually send pre-approved cards without doing an adequate credit check. Judges also discover that cards are issued to all applicants, no matter what number is entered into the household income blank on the credit application. Finally, judges are finding that debtors are using the cards for the precise reasons the creditors encouraged them to use the cards—"when you're short on cash," "to take that much-deserved vacation," "to consolidate other debts" or "to buy expensive gifts." Ultimately, most judges rule that credit card issuers must assume responsibility for their own neglectful behavior and cannot claim fraud when someone on the financial edge uses a card for precisely the reasons anticipated by the issuer.

2. Claims That the Debt Is Secured

A credit card issuer might try a different ploy if its claim of fraud doesn't get anywhere—to object to the discharge of a credit card debt by claiming that it is secured and that you must reaffirm the debt or select another option related to secured debts. (These are discussed in Chapter 5, Section C.) The creditor, rather than raise concerns at the meeting of the creditors or file a formal Complaint to Determine Dischargeability of a Debt, might simply send you a reaffirmation agreement to sign. Accompanying the agreement is a letter in which the creditor promises to reinstate your credit if the you agree to repay the debt.

An estimated 50% of creditors send reaffirmation agreements, usually to harass or frighten. It's *never* a good idea to sign a reaffirmation agreement in such a situation. Why saddle yourself with credit card debts you filed for bankruptcy to eliminate? Don't be lured by the promise of restored credit. Creditors don't restore credit until *after* the outstanding debt is paid in full. Besides, you can apply for a new credit card after your bankruptcy case is over. (See Chapter 9.) Throw the reaffirmation agreement in the garbage, or send it back after writing "Decline" across it. Ninety-nine percent of the time you'll never hear from the creditor again.

 Now is the time to complete the Chapter 6 questions on the "Should I File For Bankruptcy?" checklist.

Will I Lose My Job, Children, Freedom or Self-Respect?

For many people, the thought of filing for bankruptcy raises a number of troubling questions. Many of these have to do with eliminating debts; those are answered in Chapter 3. Other questions concern the potential loss of property; those are addressed in Chapters 4 and 5.

But many of the questions go beyond debts and assets and hit at the core of what it means to be a member of our society—earning a livelihood, parenting and retaining one's freedom and self-respect.

A. Will I Lose My Job?

The Bankruptcy Code states that the government cannot discriminate against you for having filed for bankruptcy. If you work for a local, state or government agency, you cannot be fired. Nor can your public employer take other punitive action against you, such as demote you, reduce your salary or take away responsibilities. The Bankruptcy Code also states that private employers cannot fire you or take other punitive action against you solely because you filed for bankruptcy.

In fact, it's rare that an employer ever finds out about a Chapter 7 bankruptcy filing. About the only time this might happen is if a creditor has sued you, obtained a judgment against you and started garnishing your wages. The bankruptcy will stop the wage garnishment, and your employer will be notified as such. In such a situation, your employer (or at least the payroll department) already knows you are having financial problems and will probably welcome the bankruptcy as a way for you to take affirmative steps to put your problems behind you.

On the other hand, if you file for Chapter 13 bankruptcy, your employer is most likely to learn of your bankruptcy case. This is because if you have a regular job with regular income, the bankruptcy judge may order your Chapter 13 payments to be automatically deducted from your wages and sent to the bankruptcy court. This is called an income deduction order.

You may not like the idea of the income deduction order, but the bankruptcy court is likely to deny your Chapter 13 plan if you refuse to comply with it. And realize that the order will probably make it easier for you to complete your plan. The success rate of Chapter 13 cases is higher for debtors with income deduction orders than for debtors who pay the trustee themselves.

Closely associated with many jobs is a security clearance. If you are a member of the armed forces or an employee of the CIA, FBI, another government agency or a private company that contracts with the government, you may have a security clearance. Do you risk losing your security clearance if you file for bankruptcy? Probably not—in fact, the opposite may be true. According to credit counselors for the military and the CIA, a person with financial problems—particularly someone with a lot of debt—is a high risk of being blackmailed. By filing for bankruptcy and getting rid of the debts, you substantially lower that risk. Bankruptcy usually works more in your favor than to your detriment.

WHAT ABOUT FUTURE JOBS?

While the Bankruptcy Code expressly prohibits private employers from firing you, it is unclear whether or not the act prohibits private employers from not hiring you because you went through bankruptcy. The Code is silent, and there are no cases that address the question head on. On the other hand, courts interpreting the section of the Bankruptcy Code prohibiting government discrimination have ruled that government employers cannot deny someone a job just because that person has filed for bankruptcy.

An employer is likely to find out about a past bankruptcy by doing a credit check. The federal Fair Credit Reporting Act requires that employers have your written authorization before checking your credit report. If you're asked to give such authorization, consider speaking candidly with your potential employer about what he or she will find in your file. Honesty up front about past problems that are truly behind you may outweigh the bankruptcy filing itself.

B. Can I Be Discriminated Against?

All federal, state and local governmental units are prohibited from discriminating against you solely because you filed for bankruptcy. This includes denying, revoking, suspending or refusing to renew a license, permit, charter, franchise or other similar grant. Judges interpreting this law have ruled that the government cannot:

- deny you or terminate your public benefits
- deny you or evict you from public housing
- deny you or refuse to renew your state liquor license
- exclude you from participating in a state home mortgage finance program
- withhold your college transcript
- deny you a driver's license
- deny you a contract, such as a contract for a construction project, or
- exclude you from participating in a government-guaranteed student loan program.

In general, once any government-related debt has been discharged, all acts against you that arise out of that debt also must end. If, for example, you lost your driver's license because you didn't pay a court judgment that resulted from a car accident, once the debt is discharged, you must be granted a license. If the judgment wasn't discharged, however, you can still be denied your license until you pay up.

Prohibitions against private discrimination aren't as broad as prohibitions against government discrimination. As mentioned above, private employers may not fire you or take other punitive action against you because you filed for bankruptcy. All other forms of discrimination in the private sector, however, such as denying you housing or withholding a college transcript, are legal.

C. Will I Lose My Children?

There are no reported cases from any state of a parent losing custody because he or she filed for bankruptcy. Bankruptcy and divorce (or separation) are so often related these days that one frequently follows the other. Bankruptcy judges are becoming experts on family law matters, and family law judges are becoming experts in bankruptcy. Don't worry about your bankruptcy affecting your custody status.

D. Will I Lose My Freedom?

We Americans are used to some basic freedoms, and many people fear the loss of those freedoms if they file for bankruptcy. Relax. Except in some unusual cases, this is just not going to happen.

Can I go to jail? Filing for bankruptcy is not considered a crime. You must sign your bankruptcy papers under "penalty of perjury," however, swearing that everything in them is true. If you deliberately commit any number of bad acts, such as failing to disclose property, omitting material information about your financial affairs, unloading nonexempt assets just before filing or using a false Social Security number (to hide your identity as a prior filer), you can be prosecuted for fraud.

While such prosecution is rare, it's on the rise, all across the country. A debtor in Massachusetts went to jail for failing to list on his bankruptcy papers his interest in a condominium and $26,000 worth of jewelry. Another Massachusetts debtor is serving time for listing her home on her bankruptcy papers as worth $70,000 when it had been appraised for

$116,000. An Alaska debtor was jailed for failing to disclose buried cash and diamonds. A Pennsylvania debtor omitted from her papers $50,000 from a divorce settlement and was sentenced to some time in prison.

The message is simple: bankruptcy is geared towards the honest debtor who got in too deep and needs the help of the bankruptcy court to get a fresh start. A bankruptcy judge will not help someone who has played fast and loose with creditors or tries to do so with the bankruptcy court. If you lie, hide or cheat, it will probably come back to haunt you to a far greater degree than your current debt crisis does.

Can I move? You are free to change your residence after you file. Just be sure to send the trustee a change of address form if your case is still open. If your move involves selling your house and you've filed a Chapter 13 bankruptcy, the trustee may want to use any proceeds of the sale to pay off your creditors.

Can I change jobs? You can certainly change jobs while your bankruptcy case is pending, and certainly after it ends. If you've filed a Chapter 13 case, be sure to tell the trustee so she can transfer the income deduction order.

Can I get divorced? No one can force you to stay married, not even a bankruptcy judge. If you've filed for Chapter 7 bankruptcy and want to end your marriage, go ahead. Your bankruptcy case will probably end long before your divorce case does.

If you've filed a Chapter 13 case with your spouse, you may face some complications if you want to continue your case and get divorced. Bankruptcy law states that to be eligible to file a joint case, you must be a married couple. If you divorce, you are no longer eligible to file (or maintain) a joint Chapter 13 case, at least in theory. The trustee could file a motion to dismiss your case. Some trustees have been known to ignore a divorce if both spouses want to keep the Chapter 13 going and continue to make the payments. Even so, you will probably want to ask the divorce court to divide your divorce ("bifurcate," in legalese) so that your marital status changes from married to divorced, but that the final division of marital property and debts is postponed until your Chapter 13 case ends. You could simplify matters by separating, but not divorcing. In either situation, be sure to let the trustee know of any change of address.

Who finds out? It's highly unusual for anyone to find out about your bankruptcy other than your creditors, businesses that obtain a copy of your credit report and the people you tell. Although your bankruptcy filing will be published in a local newspaper, these notices often appear in low-circulation papers. Bankruptcy filings aren't broadcast on local television or radio. No one from the bankruptcy court will visit your home or your business, even if you are self-employed. Filing for bankruptcy isn't like "getting in trouble with the IRS." Most people are in and out of the bankruptcy system in a matter of months, and find the trustee and judge (if they ever even face a judge) to be friendly and helpful.

E. Will I Lose My Self-Respect?

Americans learn almost from birth that it's a good thing to buy all sorts of goods and services. A highly paid army of persuaders surrounds us with thousands of seductive messages each day that all say "buy, buy, buy." Easily available credit makes living beyond one's means easy and resisting the siren sounds of the advertisers difficult. But we're also told that if we fail to pay for it all right on time, we're miserable deadbeats. In short, much of American economic life is built on a contradiction.

If for some reason, such as illness, loss of work or just plain bad planning, our ability to pay for the goods or services we need is interrupted, guilt is often our first feeling. We may even feel we've fundamentally failed as human beings.

Nonsense. There's more to life than an A+ credit rating, and better things to feel guilty about than the failure to pay bills on time. The importance we have for our families, friends and neighbors should never be forgotten. Nor should the fact that the American economy is based on consumer debt. Creditors expect defaults and bankruptcies and treat them as a cost of doing business. The reason so many banks issue credit cards is that it is a very profitable business, even with so many bankruptcies.

Fortunately, for thousands of years it's been recognized that debts can get the better of even the most conscientious among us. From Biblical times to the present, sane societies have discouraged debtors from falling on their swords and have provided sensible ways for debt-oppressed people to start new economic lives. In the United States, this is done through bankruptcy.

Bankruptcy is a truly worthy part of our legal system, based as it is on forgiveness rather than retribution. Certainly, it helps keep families together, reduces suicide and keeps the ranks of the homeless from growing even larger.

 Now is the time to complete the Chapter 7 questions on the "Should I File For Bankruptcy?" checklist.

Is It Too Hard to File?

Filing for bankruptcy, particularly Chapter 7 bankruptcy, can be a lot like doing your taxes. Most people can handle the process on their own. Although fewer than 25% of all bankruptcy filers are "do-it-yourselfers," in some bankruptcy courts as many as 33%-40% of people file without hiring an attorney.

Most Chapter 7 bankruptcy cases are simple. If you have only unsecured dischargeable debts and exempt property, you can probably successfully go it alone. As your case increases in complexity, however—for example, you have a lien on your house you want to wipe out or you own some valuable property that might be nonexempt—the more you may need help to achieve the best possible results under the bankruptcy laws.

By contrast, most people who file for Chapter 13 bankruptcy hire an attorney. As explained below in Section C, Chapter 13 bankruptcy is usually difficult to do pro per or pro se (Latin for "for oneself).

A. Filling Out the Bankruptcy Forms

In every bankruptcy case, you must fill out the following forms:

- Form 1—Voluntary Petition, in which you ask the bankruptcy court to discharge your debts.
- Form 6, which consists of:
  - ✓ Schedule A—Real Property
  - ✓ Schedule B—Personal Property
  - ✓ Schedule C—Property Claimed as Exempt
  - ✓ Schedule D—Creditors Holding Secured Claims
  - ✓ Schedule E—Creditors Holding Unsecured Priority Claims
  - ✓ Schedule F—Creditors Holding Unsecured Nonpriority Claims
  - ✓ Schedule G—Executory Contracts and Unexpired Leases
  - ✓ Schedule H—Codebtors
  - ✓ Schedule I—Current Income
  - ✓ Schedule J—Current Expenditures

✓ Summary Schedules A through J

✓ Declaration Concerning Debtor's Schedules, in which you declare under penalty of perjury that the information you put in the schedules is true and correct.

- Form 7—Statement of Financial Affairs, in which you provide information about your economic affairs during the past several years.

- Form 8—Chapter 7 Individual Debtor's Statement of Intention, in which you tell the court and your secured creditors what you plan to do with your property listed as collateral for a secured loan. (Chapter 7 bankruptcy only.)

- Mailing matrix, on which you list your creditors and their addresses.

- Chapter 13 Repayment Plan, on which you propose your repayment plan to the bankruptcy court. (Chapter 13 bankruptcy only.)

Although you are not required to type your forms, many courts prefer that they be typed. But even if your court doesn't, the court clerk is likely to be friendlier if you show up with neatly typed forms.

The following tips might help you determine whether or not you want to file for bankruptcy on your own:

- **You must be ridiculously thorough.** Always err on the side of giving too much information rather than too little.

- **You must respond to every question.** If a question that doesn't apply to you doesn't have a "none" box to check, you will have to type in "N/A" for "not applicable."

- **You will repeat yourself.** Sometimes different forms—or different questions on the same form—ask for the same or overlapping information. You will have to provide the same information multiple times.

- **You must be scrupulously honest.** As explained in Chapter 7, you must swear, under penalty of perjury, that you've been truthful on your bankruptcy forms. The most likely consequence for failing to be scrupulously honest is a dismissal of your bankruptcy case, but you could be prosecuted for perjury if it's evident that you deliberately lied.

Below are samples of the court forms filed in a typical Chapter 7 bankruptcy. These are the same forms filed in a Chapter 13 case (minus

Form 8). Chapter 13 bankruptcy also requires a repayment plan. There is no official Chapter 13 plan form that all bankruptcy courts use, so included below are a few copies of completed Chapter 13 plans. Review the forms carefully. If you think you can complete them easily on your own with the help of a good self-help book, then bankruptcy shouldn't be too hard for you.

FORM 1. VOLUNTARY PETITION

UNITED STATES BANKRUPTCY COURT <u>Northern</u> DISTRICT OF <u>Ohio, Eastern Division</u>	**Voluntary Petition**

Name of Debtor (if individual, enter Last, First, Middle): MAYTAG, MOLLY MARIA	Name of Joint Debtor (Spouse) (Last, First, Middle): MAYTAG, JONATHAN
All Other Names used by the Debtor in the last 6 years (include married, maiden, and trade names): Johnson, Molly Maria	All Other Names used by the Joint Debtor in the last 6 years (include married, maiden, and trade names): Maytag Delicatessen
Soc. Sec./Tax I.D. No. (if more than one, state all): 999-99-9999	Soc. Sec./Tax I.D. No. (if more than one, state all): 000-00-0000
Street Address of Debtor (No. & Street, City, State & Zip Code): 21 Scarborough Road South Cleveland Hights, OH 41118	Street Address of Joint Debtor (No. & Street, City, State & Zip Code): 21 Scarborough Road South Cleveland Hights, OH 41118
County of Residence or of the Principal Place of Business: Cuyahoga	County of Residence or of the Principal Place of Business: Cuyahoga
Mailing Address of Debtor (if different from street address): N/A	Mailing Address of Joint Debtor (if different from street address): N/A

Location of Principal Assets of Business Debtor
(if different from street address above):
N/A

Information Regarding the Debtor (Check the Applicable Boxes)

Venue (Check any applicable box)

☒ Debtor has been domiciled or has had a residence, principal place of business, or principal assets in this District for 180 days immediately preceding the date of this petition or for a longer part of such 180 days than in any other District.

☐ There is a bankruptcy case concerning debtor's affiliate, general partner, or partnership pending in this District.

Type of Debtor (Check all boxes that apply)		**Chapter or Section of Bankruptcy Code Under Which the Petition is Filed** (Check one box)
☒ Individual(s) ☐ Railroad		☒ Chapter 7 ☐ Chapter 11 ☐ Chapter 13
☐ Corporation ☐ Stockbroker		☐ Chapter 9 ☐ Chapter 12
☐ Partnership ☐ Commodity Broker		☐ Sec. 304 – Case ancillary to foreign proceeding
☐ Other _____		

Nature of Debts (Check one box)	**Filing Fee** (Check one box)
☒ Consumer/Non-Business ☐ Business	☒ Full Filing Fee attached
Chapter 11 Small Business (Check all boxes that apply)	☐ Filing Fee to be paid in installments. (Applicable to individuals only.) Must attach signed application for the court's consideration certifying that the debtor is unable to pay fee except in installments. Rule 1006(b). See Official Form No. 3.
☐ Debtor is a small business as defined in 11 U.S.C. § 101 ☐ Debtor is and elects to be considered a small business under 11 U.S.C. §1121(e) (Optional)	

Statistical/Administrative Information (Estimates only)	THIS SPACE FOR COURT USE ONLY
☒ Debtor estimates that funds will be available for distribution to unsecured creditors. ☐ Debtor estimates that, after any exempt property is excluded and administrative expenses paid, there will be no funds available for distribution to unsecured creditors.	

Estimated Number of Creditors	1-15	16-49	50-99	100-199	200-999	1000-over
	☐	☒	☐	☐	☐	☐

Estimated Assets							
$0 to $50,000	$50,001 to $100,000	$100,001 to $500,000	$500,001 to $1 million	$1,000,001 to $10 million	$10,000,001 to $50 million	$50,000,001 to $100 million	More than $100 million
☐	☒	☐	☐	☐	☐	☐	☐

Estimated Debts							
$0 to $50,000	$50,001 to $100,000	$100,001 to $500,000	$500,001 to $1 million	$1,000,001 to $10 million	$10,000,001 to $50 million	$50,000,001 to $100 million	More than $100 million
☐	☒	☐	☐	☐	☐	☐	☐

Voluntary Petition
(This page must be completed and filed in every case.)

Name of Debtor(s): **Maytag, Molly & Jonathan**   Form 1, Page 2

Prior Bankruptcy Case Filed Within Last 6 Years (If more than one, attach additional sheet)		
Location Where Filed: **N/A**	Case Number:	Date Filed:

Pending Bankruptcy Case Filed by any Spouse, Partner or Affiliate of this Debtor (If more than one, attach additional sheet)		
Name of Debtor: **N/A**	Case Number:	Date Filed:
District:	Relationship:	Judge:

Signatures

Signature(s) of Debtor(s) (Individual/Joint)

I declare under penalty of perjury that the information provided in this petition is true and correct.

[If petitioner is an individual whose debts are primarily consumer debts and has chosen to file under chapter 7] I am aware that I may proceed under chapter 7, 11, 12 or 13 of title 11, United States Code, understand the relief available under each such chapter, and choose to proceed under chapter 7. I request relief in accordance with the chapter of title 11, United States Code, specified in this petition.

X *Molly Maytag*
Signature of Debtor

X *Jonathan Maytag*
Signature of Joint Debtor

(216) 555-7373
Telephone Number (If not represented by attorney)

July 13, 20XX
Date

Signature of Debtor (Corporation/Partnership)

I declare under penalty of perjury that the information provided in this petition is true and correct and that I have been authorized to file this petition on behalf of the debtor.

The debtor requests relief in accordance with the chapter of title 11, United States Code, specified in this petition.

X _____**N/A**_____
Signature of Authorized Individual

_____
Printed Name of Authorized Individual

_____
Title of Authorized Individual

_____
Date

Signature of Attorney

X ___**N/A**___
Signature of Attorney for Debtor(s)

_____
Printed Name of Attorney for Debtor(s)

_____
Firm Name

_____
Address

_____

_____
Telephone Number

_____
Date

Exhibit A

(To be completed if debtor is required to file periodic reports (e.g., forms 10K and 10Q) with the Securities and Exchange Commission pursuant to Section 13 or 15(d) of the Securities Exchange Act of 1934 and is requesting relief under chapter 11.)

☐ Exhibit A is attached and made a part of this petition.

Exhibit B

(To be completed if debtor is an individual whose debts are primarily consumer debts.)

I, the attorney for the petitioner named in the foregoing petition, declare that I have informed the petitioner that [he or she] may proceed under chapter 7, 11, 12, or 13 of title 11, United States Code, and have explained the relief available under each such chapter.

X ___**N/A**___
Signature of Attorney for Debtor(s)   Date

Signature of Non-Attorney Petition Preparer

I certify that I am a bankruptcy petition preparer as defined in 11 U.S.C. § 110, that I prepared this document for compensation, and that I have provided the debtor with a copy of this document.

N/A
Printed Name of Bankruptcy Petition Preparer

_____
Social Security Number

_____
Address

_____

Names and Social Security numbers of all other individuals who prepared or assisted in preparing this document:

N/A

If more than one person prepared this document, attach additional sheets conforming to the appropriate official form for each person.

X _____
Signature of Bankruptcy Petition Preparer

_____
Date

A bankruptcy petition preparer's failure to comply with the provisions of title 11 and the Federal Rules of Bankruptcy Procedure may result in fines or imprisonment or both. 11 U.S.C. § 110; 18 U.S.C. § 156.

In re _Maytag, Molly and Jonathan_ ,
  Debtor

Case No._____
  (If known)

SCHEDULE A—REAL PROPERTY

Except as directed below, list all real property in which the debtor has any legal, equitable, or future interest, including all property owned as a co-tenant, community property, or in which the debtor has a life estate. Include any property in which the debtor holds rights and powers exercisable for the debtor's own benefit. If the debtor is married, state whether husband, wife, or both own the property by placing an "H," "W," "J," or "C" in the column labeled "Husband, Wife, Joint, or Community." If the debtor holds no interest in real property, write "None" under "Description and Location of Property."

Do not include interests in executory contracts and unexpired leases on this schedule. List them in Schedule G—Executory Contracts and Unexpired Leases.

If an entity claims to have a lien or hold a secured interest in any property, state the amount of the secured claim. See Schedule D. If no entity claims to hold a secured interest in the property, write "None" in the column labeled "Amount of Secured Claim."

If the debtor is an individual or if a joint petition is filed, state the amount of any exception claimed in the property only in Schedule C—Property Claimed as Exempt.

DESCRIPTION AND LOCATION OF PROPERTY	NATURE OF DEBTOR'S INTEREST IN PROPERTY	HUSBAND, WIFE, JOINT, OR COMMUNITY	CURRENT MARKET VALUE OF DEBTOR'S INTEREST IN PROPERTY WITHOUT DEDUCTING ANY SECURED CLAIM OR EXEMPTION	AMOUNT OF SECURED CLAIM
Residence at 21 Scarborough Road South, Cleveland Heights, OH 44118	Fee Simple	J	$95,000	$75,000 mortgage $12,000 second mortgage $2,000 judgment lien
Unimproved lot at 244 Highway 50, Parma, OH 44000	Fee Simple	H	$5,000	none

Total ➡ $ 100,000

(Report also on Summary of Schedules.)

In re ___Maytag, Molly and Jonathan_____ , Case No._____
    Debtor   (If known)

SCHEDULE B—PERSONAL PROPERTY

Except as directed below, list all personal property of the debtor of whatever kind. If the debtor has no property in one or more of the categories, place an "X" in the appropriate position in the column labeled "None." If additional space is needed in any category, attach a separate sheet properly identified with the case name, case number, and the number of the category. If the debtor is married, state whether husband, wife, or both own the property by placing an "H," "W," "J," or "C" in the column labeled "Husband, Wife, Joint, or Community." If the debtor is an individual or a joint petition is filed, state the amount of any exemptions claimed only in Schedule C—Property Claimed as Exempt.

Do not include interests in executory contracts and unexpired leases on this schedule. List them in Schedule G—Executory Contracts and Unexpired Leases.

If the property is being held for the debtor by someone else, state that person's name and address under "Description and Location of Property."

TYPE OF PROPERTY	NONE	* All property is located at our residence unless otherwise noted. DESCRIPTION AND LOCATION OF PROPERTY	HUSBAND, WIFE, JOINT, OR COMMUNITY	CURRENT MARKET VALUE OF DEBTOR'S INTEREST IN PROPERTY, WITHOUT DEDUCTING ANY SECURED CLAIM OR EXEMPTION
1. Cash on hand.		Cash from wages	J	100
2. Checking, savings or other financial accounts, certificates of deposit, or shares in banks, savings and loan, thrift, building and loan, and homestead associations, or credit unions, brokerage houses, or cooperatives.		Checking account #12345, Ameritrust, 10 Financial Way, Cleveland Hts, OH 44118 (from wages)	J	250
		Savings account #98765, Shaker Savings, 44 Trust Street, Cleveland Hts, OH 44118 (from wages)	J	400
		Checking account #058-118061, Ohio Savings, 1818 Lakeshore Dr., Cleveland, OH 44123	H	100
3. Security deposits with public utilities, telephone companies, landlords, and others.	X			
4. Household goods and furnishings, including audio, video, and computer equipment.		Stereo system	J	300
		Washer/Dryer set	J	150
		Refrigerator	J	250
		Stove	J	150
		Household furniture	J	600
		Minor appliances	J	75
		Antique desk	J	250
		Vacuum	J	30
		Bed & bedding	J	500
		Television	J	135
		VCR	J	75
		Lawnmower	J	100
		Swingset, children's toys	J	180
		Snowblower	J	100
		Oriental rug	J	2,500

In re **Maytag Molly and Jonathan**   ,   Case No._____
           Debtor   (If known)

SCHEDULE B—PERSONAL PROPERTY
(Continuation Sheet)

TYPE OF PROPERTY	NONE	DESCRIPTION AND LOCATION OF PROPERTY	HUSBAND, WIFE, JOINT, OR COMMUNITY	CURRENT MARKET VALUE OF DEBTOR'S INTEREST IN PROPERTY, WITHOUT DEDUCTING ANY SECURED CLAIM OR EXEMPTION
5. Books, pictures and other art objects, antiques, stamp, coin, record, tape, compact disc, and other collections or collectibles.		Books Stamp collection	J J	50 75
6. Wearing apparel.		Clothing	J	625
7. Furs and jewelry.		Wedding rings Diamond necklace Watches	J W J	225 325 50
8. Firearms and sports, photographic, and other hobby equipment.		Mountain bike Camera Sword collection	J J W	165 125 1,485
9. Interests in insurance policies. Name insurance company of each policy and itemize surrender or refund value of each.		Life insurance policy, Lively Ins. Co., 120 Manhattan Street, NY, NY 10012 Policy #14-171136 Life insurance policy, Live-a-long-time Co., 52 Mitchell Ave., Hartford, CT 06434. Policy #33-19195WY17	H W	120 65
10. Annuities. Itemize and name each issuer.	X			
11. Interests in IRA, ERISA, Keogh, or other pension or profit sharing plans. Itemize.		Cleveland Builder's Pension, 100 Chester Way, Cleveland, OH 44114 IRA, Basic Bank, 9712 Smitco Creek Blvd., Columbus, OH 45923	H J	6,612 3,400
12. Stock and interests in incorporated and unincorporated businesses. Itemize.		Trusso Corp. stock, #3711. 50 shares @ $20 each Investco Ltd. stock, #1244711, 5 shares @ $100 each Rayco Co. stock, #RC53, 20 shares @ $40 each All certificates at Ameritrust, 10 Financial Way, Cleveland Hts, OH 44118	J J J	1,000 500 800
13. Interests in partnerships or joint ventures. Itemize.	X			

In re _____ Maytag, Molly and Jonathan _____,   Case No._____
          Debtor   (If known)

SCHEDULE B—PERSONAL PROPERTY
(Continuation Sheet)

TYPE OF PROPERTY	NONE	DESCRIPTION AND LOCATION OF PROPERTY	HUSBAND, WIFE, JOINT, OR COMMUNITY	CURRENT MARKET VALUE OF DEBTOR'S INTEREST IN PROPERTY, WITHOUT DEDUCTING ANY SECURED CLAIM OR EXEMPTION
14. Government and corporate bonds and other negotiable and non-negotiable instruments.		US Savings Bonds, located at Ameritrust, 10 Financial Way, Cleveland Hts, OH 44118	J	1,000
		Promissory note from Jonathan Maytag's sister, Trini Maytag Ellison, dated 11/3/XX	J	500
15. Accounts receivable.	X			
16. Alimony, maintenance, support, and property settlements to which the debtor is or may be entitled. Give particulars.	X			
17. Other liquidated debts owing debtor including tax refunds. Give particulars.		Wages for 6/XX from Cleveland Builder	H	1,900
		Wages for 6/1/XX to 6/30/XX from Typing Circles	W	100
18. Equitable or future interest, life estates, and rights or powers exercisable for the benefit of the debtor other than those listed in Schedule of Real Property.	X			
19. Contingent and noncontingent interests in estate of a decedent, death benefit plan, life insurance policy, or trust.	X			
20. Other contingent and unliquidated claims of every nature, including tax refunds, counterclaims of the debtor, and rights to setoff claims. Give estimated value of each.	X			
21. Patents, copyrights, and other intellectual property. Give particulars.	X			
22. Licenses, franchises, and other general intangibles. Give particulars.	X			

In re ___Maytag, Molly and Jonathan___,   Case No._____
                     Debtor   (If known)

SCHEDULE B—PERSONAL PROPERTY
(Continuation Sheet)

TYPE OF PROPERTY	NONE	DESCRIPTION AND LOCATION OF PROPERTY	HUSBAND, WIFE, JOINT, OR COMMUNITY	CURRENT MARKET VALUE OF DEBTOR'S INTEREST IN PROPERTY, WITHOUT DEDUCTING ANY SECURED CLAIM OR EXEMPTION
23. Automobiles, trucks, trailers, and other vehicles and accessories.		1988 Honda Motorcycle	W	1,000
24. Boats, motors, and accessories.		Sailboard, docked at Lake Erie Dock, Cleveland, OH	J	1,250
25. Aircraft and accessories.	X			
26. Office equipment, furnishings, and supplies.		Computer (for business)	J	1,100
		Typewriter (for business)	J	125
		Fax Machine (for business)	J	500
27. Machinery, fixtures, equipment, and supplies used in business.		Carpentry tools	J	150
28. Inventory.	X			
29. Animals.		Poodles (2)	J	200
30. Crops—growing or harvested. Give particulars.	X			
31. Farming equipment and implements.	X			
32. Farm supplies, chemicals, and feed.	X			
33. Other personal property of any kind not already listed, such as season tickets. Itemize.				

Total ➡ $ 29,692

___0___ continuation sheets attached

(Include amounts from any continuation sheets attached. Report total also on Summary of Schedules.)

8/12   Bankruptcy: Is It the Right Solution to Your Debt Problems?

In re Maytag, Molly and Jonathan   ,   Case No._____
         Debtor   (If known)

SCHEDULE C—PROPERTY CLAIMED AS EXEMPT

Debtor elects the exemptions to which debtor is entitled under:

(Check one box)

☐ 11 U.S.C. § 522(b)(1): Exemptions provided in 11 U.S.C. § 522(d). **Note: These exemptions are available only in certain states.**

☒ 11 U.S.C. § 522(b)(2): Exemptions available under applicable nonbankruptcy federal laws, state or local law where the debtor's domicile has been located for the 180 days immediately preceding the filing of the petition, or for a longer portion of the 180-day period than in any other place, and the debtor's interest as a tenant by the entirety or joint tenant to the extent the interest is exempt from process under applicable nonbankruptcy law.

DESCRIPTION OF PROPERTY	SPECIFY LAW PROVIDING EACH EXEMPTION	VALUE OF CLAIMED EXEMPTION	CURRENT MARKET VALUE OF PROPERTY WITHOUT DEDUCTING EXEMPTIONS
Real Property Residence at 21 Scarborough Road South, Cleveland Hts, OH 44118	2329.66(A)(1)	10,000	95,000
Cash on hand Cash from wages	2329.66(A)(13)	100	100
Money deposits Ameritrust checking account #12345	2329.66(A)(4)(a)	250	250
Shaker Savings account #98765	2329.66(A)(4)(a)	400	400
Ohio Savings account #058-118061	1775.24(A)(4)(a)	100	100
Household goods Stereo System	2329.66(A)(17) (wildcard)	300	300
Washer/Dryer set	2329.66(A)(4)(b)	150	150
Refrigerator	2329.66(A)(3)	250	250
Stove	2329.66(A)(3)	150	150
Household furniture	2329.66(A)(4)(b)	600	600
Minor appliances	2329.66(A)(4)(b)	75	75
Antique desk	2329.66(A)(4)(b)	250	250
Vacuum	2329.66(A)(4)(b)	30	30
Beds & bedding	2329.66(A)(3)	500	500
Television	2329.66(A)(4)	135	135
VCR	2329.66(A)(4)	75	75
Lawnmower	2329.66(A)(4)	100	100
Swingset, children's toys	2329.66(A)(4)	180	180
Snowblower	2329.66(A)(4)	100	100
Books, pictures, etc. Stamp collection	2329.66(A)(4)(b)	75	75
Lithograph	2329.66(A)(4)(b)	50	50

Because we are married, we each claim a full set of exemptions to the extent permitted by law. All references are to Ohio Revised Code unless otherwise noted.

In re Maytag, Molly and Jonathan

SCHEDULE C—PROPERTY CLAIMED AS EXEMPT

(Continuation Sheet)

DESCRIPTION OF PROPERTY	SPECIFY LAW PROVIDING EACH EXEMPTION	VALUE OF CLAIMED EXEMPTION	CURRENT MARKET VALUE OF PROPERTY WITHOUT DEDUCTING EXEMPTIONS
Wearing Apparel			
Clothing	2329.66(A)(3)	625	625
Furs & jewelry			
Wedding rings	2329.66(A)(4)(c)	225	225
Diamond necklace	2329.66(A)(4)(c)	325	325
Watches	2329.66(A)(4)(c)	50	50
Insurance			
Lively Insurance Co., life insurance policy #14-171136	3911.12	120	120
Live-a-long-time Co., life insurance policy #33-19195WY17	3911.14	65	65
IRA, Pensions, Etc.			
Cleveland Builder Pension	2329.66(A)(10)(a)	6,612	6,612
IRA	2329.66(A)(10)(b)	3,400	3,400
Firearms, sports equipment			
Mountain bike	2329.66(A)(4)(b)	165	165
Camera	2329.66(A)(4)(b)	125	125
Other liquidated debts			
Wages from Cleveland Builder	2329.66(A)(13)	1,900	1,900
Wages from Typing Circles	2329.66(A)(13)	100	100
Vehicles			
1988 Honda motorcycle	2329.66(A)(2)	1,000	1,000
Animals			
2 Poodles	2329.66(A)(4)(b)	200	200
Office equipment			
Computer (for business)	2329.66(A)(5)	1,100	1,100
Typewriter (for business)	2329.66(A)(5)	125	125
Fax (for business)	2329.66(A)(17) (wildcard)	500	500
Tools of trade			
Carpentry tools	2329.66(A)(5)	150	150

In re **Maytag, Molly and Jonathan** _____, Case No._____

Debtor   (If known)

SCHEDULE D—CREDITORS HOLDING SECURED CLAIMS

State the name, mailing address, including zip code, and account number, if any, of all entities holding claims secured by property of the debtor as of the date of filing of the petition. List creditors holding all types of secured interest such as judgment liens, garnishments, statutory liens, mortgages, deeds of trust, and other security interests. List creditors in alphabetical order to the extent practicable. If all secured creditors will not fit on this page, use the continuation sheet provided.

If any entity other than a spouse in a joint case may be jointly liable on a claim, place an "X" in the column labeled "Codebtor," include the entity on the appropriate schedule of creditors, and complete Schedule H—Codebtors. If a joint petition is filed, state whether husband, wife, both of them, or the marital community may be liable on each claim by placing an "H," "W," "J," or "C" in the column labeled "Husband, Wife, Joint, or Community."

If the claim is contingent, place an "X" in the column labeled "Contingent." If the claim is unliquidated, place an "X" in the column labeled "Unliquidated." If the claim is disputed, place an "X" in the column labeled "Disputed." (You may need to place an "X" in more than one of these three columns.)

Report the total of all claims listed on this schedule in the box labeled "Total" on the last sheet of the completed schedule. Report this total also on the Summary of Schedules.

☐ Check this box if debtor has no creditors holding secured claims to report on this Schedule D.

CREDITOR'S NAME AND MAILING ADDRESS INCLUDING ZIP CODE	CODEBTOR	HUSBAND, WIFE, JOINT, OR COMMUNITY	DATE CLAIM WAS INCURRED, NATURE OF LIEN, AND DESCRIPTION AND MARKET VALUE OF PROPERTY SUBJECT TO LIEN	CONTINGENT	UNLIQUIDATED	DISPUTED	AMOUNT OF CLAIM WITHOUT DEDUCTING VALUE OF COLLATERAL	UNSECURED PORTION, IF ANY
ACCOUNT NO. 64-112-1861 Ameritrust 10 Financial Way Cleveland Hts, OH 44118		J	9/12/XX; purchase-money secured debt; mortgage on residence VALUE $ 95,000				75,000	-0-
ACCOUNT NO. 64-112-8423 Ameritrust 10 Financial Way Cleveland Hts, OH 44118		J	8/9/XX; nonpurchase-money secured debt; second mortgage on residence VALUE $ 95,000				12,000	-0-
ACCOUNT NO. N/A Computers for Sale P.O. Box 1183 San Ramon, CA 94000		J	8/12/XX; purchase-money secured interest, computer VALUE $ 1,100				2,000	900
ACCOUNT NO. 521129 Quality Collection Agency 21 Main Drive West Cleveland Hts, OH 44115	"		" VALUE $				"	"

_____1_____ continuation sheets attached

Subtotal ➡ (Total of this page) $ 89,000

Total ➡ (Use only on last page) $ N/A

(Report total also on Summary of Schedules)

In re _Maytag, Molly and Jonathan_____, Case No._____
　　　　　　　　　　Debtor　　　　　　　　　　　　　　　(If known)

SCHEDULE D—CREDITORS HOLDING SECURED CLAIMS
(Continuation Sheet)

CREDITOR'S NAME AND MAILING ADDRESS INCLUDING ZIP CODE	CODEBTOR	HUSBAND, WIFE, JOINT, OR COMMUNITY	DATE CLAIM WAS INCURRED, NATURE OF LIEN, AND DESCRIPTION AND MARKET VALUE OF PROPERTY SUBJECT TO LIEN	CONTINGENT	UNLIQUIDATED	DISPUTED	AMOUNT OF CLAIM WITHOUT DEDUCTING VALUE OF COLLATERAL	UNSECURED PORTION, IF ANY
ACCOUNT NO. 5514 Fanny's Furniture 14–4th Street Cleveland, OH 44114		J	6/4/XX; purchase-money secured interest, children's bedroom furniture VALUE $ 450				1,000	500
ACCOUNT NO. N/A Bonnie Johnson 40 Mayfield University Hts, OH 44118		X	" VALUE $				"	"
ACCOUNT NO. 834-19-77381 Ohio Savings 100 Chester Way Cleveland, OH 44115		J	9/1/XX; judgment lien on all real property in Cuyahoga county VALUE $ 100,000				2,200	-0-
ACCOUNT NO. N/A George Money, Attorney 10 Main Drive Street Cleveland, OH 44112		"	" VALUE $				"	"
ACCOUNT NO. VALUE $								
ACCOUNT NO. VALUE $								

Subtotal ➡ (Total of this page) $ 3,200

Total ➡ (Use only on last page) $ 92,200

Sheet no. _1_ of _1_ continuation sheets attached to
Schedule of Creditors Holding Secured Claims

(Report total also on Summary of Schedules)

In re ___Maytag, Molly and Jonathan_____,   Case No._____
                    Debtor   (If known)

SCHEDULE E—CREDITORS HOLDING UNSECURED PRIORITY CLAIMS

A complete list of claims entitled to priority, listed separately by type of priority, is to be set forth on the sheets provided. Only holders of unsecured claims entitled to priority should be listed in this schedule. In the boxes provided on the attached sheets, state the name and mailing address, including zip code, and account number, if any, of all entities holding priority claims against the debtor or the property of the debtor, as of the date of the filing of the petition.

If any entity other than a spouse in a joint case may be jointly liable on a claim, place an "X" in the column labeled "Codebtor," include the entity on the appropriate schedule of creditors, and complete Schedule H—Codebtors. If a joint petition is filed, state whether husband, wife, both of them, or the marital community may be liable on each claim by placing an "H," "W," "J," or "C" in the column labeled "Husband, Wife, Joint, or Community."

If the claim is contingent, place an "X" in the column labeled "Contingent." If the claim is unliquidated, place an "X" in the column labeled "Unliquidated." If the claim is disputed, place an "X" in the column labeled "Disputed." (You may need to place an "X" in more than one of these three columns.)

Report the total of all claims listed on each sheet in the box labeled "Subtotal" on each sheet. Report the total of all claims listed on this Schedule E in the box labeled "Total" on the last sheet of the completed schedule. Repeat this total also on the Summary of Schedules.

☐ **Check this box if debtor has no creditors holding unsecured priority claims to report on this Schedule E.**

TYPES OF PRIORITY CLAIMS (Check the appropriate box(es) below if claims in that category are listed on the attached sheets)

☐ **Extensions of credit in an involuntary case**

Claims arising in the ordinary course of the debtor's business or financial affairs after the commencement of the case but before the earlier of the appointment of a trustee or the order for relief. 11 U.S.C. § 507(a)(2).

☐ **Wages, salaries, and commissions**

Wages, salaries, and commissions, including vacation, severance, and sick leave pay owing to employees and commissions owing to qualifying independent sales representatives up to $4,300* per person, earned within 90 days immediately preceding the filing of the original petition, or the cessation of business, whichever occurred first, to the extent provided in 11 U.S.C. § 507(a)(3).

☐ **Contributions to employee benefit plans**

Money owed to employee benefit plans for services rendered within 180 days immediately preceding the filing of the original petition, or the cessation of business, whichever occurred first, to the extent provided in 11 U.S.C. § 507(a)(4).

☐ **Certain farmers and fishermen**

Claims of certain farmers and fishermen, up to a maximum of $4,300* per farmer or fisherman, against the debtor, as provided in 11 U.S.C. § 507(a)(5).

☐ **Deposits by individuals**

Claims of individuals up to a maximum of $1,950* for deposits for the purchase, lease, or rental of property or services for personal, family, or household use, that were not delivered or provided. 11 U.S.C. § 507(a)(6).

☐ **Alimony, Maintenance, or Support**

Claims of a spouse, former spouse, or child of the debtor for alimony, maintenance, or support, to the extent provided in 11 U.S.C. § 507(a)(7).

X **Taxes and Certain Other Debts Owed to Governmental Units**

Taxes, customs, duties, and penalties owing to federal, state, and local governmental units as set forth in 11 U.S.C. § 507(a)(8).

☐ **Commitments to Maintain the Capital of an Insured Depository Institution**

Claims based on commitments to the FDIC, RTC, Director of the Office of Thrift Supervision, Comptroller of the Currency, or Board of Governors of the Federal Reserve system, or their predecessors or successors, to maintain the capital of an insured depository institution. 11 U.S.C. § 507 (a)(9).

* Amounts are subject to adjustment on April 1, 1998, and every three years thereafter with respect to cases commenced on or after the date of adjustment.

___1___ continuation sheets attached

In re   Maytag, Molly and Jonathan   ,   Case No._____
                    Debtor   (If known)

SCHEDULE E—CREDITORS HOLDING UNSECURED PRIORITY CLAIMS
(Continuation Sheet)

Taxes
TYPE OF PRIORITY

Taxes CREDITOR'S NAME AND MAILING ADDRESS INCLUDING ZIP CODE	CODEBTOR	HUSBAND, WIFE, JOINT, OR COMMUNITY	DATE CLAIM WAS INCURRED AND CONSIDERATION FOR CLAIM	CONTINGENT	UNLIQUIDATED	DISPUTED	TOTAL AMOUNT OF CLAIM	AMOUNT ENTITLED TO PRIORITY
ACCOUNT NO. N/A IRS Cincinnati, OH 42111		J	April 15, 20XX, Tax Liability				2,200	2,200
ACCOUNT NO. N/A Ohio Dept. of Tax P.O. Box 1460 Cincinnati, OH 43266-0106		J	April 15, 20XX, Tax Liability				800	800
ACCOUNT NO.								
ACCOUNT NO.								
ACCOUNT NO.								

Subtotal ➡ (Total of this page) $ 3,000

Sheet no. __1__ of __1__ sheets attached to
Schedule of Creditors Holding Unsecured Priority Claims

Total ➡ (Use only on last page) $ 3,000
(Report total also on Summary of Schedules)

In re ___Maytag, Molly and Jonathan___,   Case No._____
_____Debtor_____   (If known)

SCHEDULE F—CREDITORS HOLDING UNSECURED NONPRIORITY CLAIMS

State the name, mailing address, including zip code, and account number, if any, of all entities holding unsecured claims without priority against the debtor or the property of the debtor as of the date of filing of the petition. Do not include claims listed in Schedules D and E. If all creditors will not fit on this page, use the continuation sheet provided.

If any entity other than a spouse in a joint case may be jointly liable on a claim, place an "X" in the column labeled "Codebtor," include the entity on the appropriate schedule of creditors, and complete Schedule H—Codebtors. If a joint petition is filed, state whether husband, wife, both of them, or the marital community may be liable on each claim by placing an "H," "W," "J," or "C" in the column labeled "Husband, Wife, Joint, or Community."

If the claim is contingent, place an "X" in the column labeled "Contingent." If the claim is unliquidated, place an "X" in the column labeled "Unliquidated." If the claim is disputed, place an "X" in the column labeled "Disputed." (You may need to place an "X" in more than one of these three columns.)

Report the total of all claims listed on this schedule in the box labeled "Total" on the last sheet of the completed schedule. Report this total also on the Summary of Schedules.

☐ Check this box if debtor has no creditors holding unsecured nonpriority claims to report on this Schedule F.

CREDITOR'S NAME AND MAILING ADDRESS INCLUDING ZIP CODE	CODEBTOR	HUSBAND, WIFE, JOINT, OR COMMUNITY	DATE CLAIM WAS INCURRED AND CONSIDERATION FOR CLAIM. IF CLAIM IS SUBJECT TO SETOFF, SO STATE	CONTINGENT	UNLIQUIDATED	DISPUTED	AMOUNT OF CLAIM
ACCOUNT NO. N/A Alan Accountant 5 Green St. Cleveland, OH 44118		J	4/XX, tax preparation				250
ACCOUNT NO. 4189000026113 American Allowance P.O. Box 1 New York, NY 10001		J	1/XX to 4/XX, VISA credit card charges			X	5,600
ACCOUNT NO. Patricia Washington, Esq. Washington & Lincoln Legal Plaza, Suite 1 Cleveland, OH 44114		"	"			"	"
ACCOUNT NO. 845061-86-3 Citibank 200 East North Columbus, OH 43266		J	20XX, student loan charges				10,000

___2___ continuation sheets attached

Subtotal ➡ (Total of this page) $ 15,850

Total ➡ (Use only on last page) $ N/A

(Report total also on Summary of Schedules)

In re ___Maytag, Molly and Jonathan___,   Case No._____
                    Debtor   (If known)

SCHEDULE F—CREDITORS HOLDING UNSECURED NONPRIORITY CLAIMS
(Continuation Sheet)

CREDITOR'S NAME AND MAILING ADDRESS INCLUDING ZIP CODE	CODEBTOR	HUSBAND, WIFE, JOINT, OR COMMUNITY	DATE CLAIM WAS INCURRED AND CONSIDERATION FOR CLAIM. IF CLAIM IS SUBJECT TO SETOFF, SO STATE	CONTINGENT	UNLIQUIDATED	DISPUTED	AMOUNT OF CLAIM
ACCOUNT NO. 9816-12HH Cleveland Hospital 19–1st Avenue Cleveland, OH 44115		J	12/XX, surgery and medical treatment				17,450
ACCOUNT NO. Jane Jackson, Esq. 50–2nd Avenue Cleveland, OH 44115		"	"				"
ACCOUNT NO. 4401 Dr. Dennis Dentist 4 Superior Way Cleveland Hts, OH 44118		W	12/XX to 6/XX, dental work				1,050
ACCOUNT NO. 222387941 Illuminating Co. 55 Public Square Cleveland, OH 44115		J	3/XX to 7/XX, electrical work				750
ACCOUNT NO. N/A Bonnie Johnson 40 Mayfield University Hts, OH 44118			8/XX, personal loan				5,500

Subtotal ➡ $ 24,750
(Total of this page)

Sheet no. __1__ of __2__ continuation sheets attached to
Schedule of Creditors Holding Unsecured Nonpriorty Claims

Total ➡ $ N/A
(Use only on last page)

(Report total also on Summary of Schedules)

In re _Maytag, Molly and Jonathan_ ,   Case No._____
          Debtor   (If known)

SCHEDULE F—CREDITORS HOLDING UNSECURED NONPRIORITY CLAIMS
(Continuation Sheet)

CREDITOR'S NAME AND MAILING ADDRESS INCLUDING ZIP CODE	CODEBTOR	HUSBAND, WIFE, JOINT, OR COMMUNITY	DATE CLAIM WAS INCURRED AND CONSIDERATION FOR CLAIM. IF CLAIM IS SUBJECT TO SETOFF, SO STATE	CONTINGENT	UNLIQUIDATED	DISPUTED	AMOUNT OF CLAIM
ACCOUNT NO. N/A Dr. Helen Jones 11 Marks Way Cleveland, OH 44112		J	4/XX to 8/XX, pediatric care				2,000
ACCOUNT NO. 11210550 Ohio Gas Company East 1717 East 9th St. Cleveland, OH 44115		J	12/XX to 6/XX, gas service				800
ACCOUNT NO. N/A Ellen Rogers 900 Grand View Jackson, WY 83001		H	6/XX to 8/XX, child support				1,800
ACCOUNT NO. 487310097 Sears P.O. Box 11 Chicago, IL 60619		J	20XX to 20XY, dept. store and catalogue charges				3,800
ACCOUNT NO. 6007 John White, Esq. 21 Main Street Cleveland, OH 44114		W	2/XX to 6/XX; represented us in lawsuits against us for unpaid bills				3,450

Subtotal ➡ (Total of this page) $ 11,850

Total ➡ (Use only on last page) $ 52,450

Sheet no. __2__ of __2__ continuation sheets attached to
Schedule of Creditors Holding Unsecured Nonpriority Claims

(Report total also on Summary of Schedules)

In re ___Maytag, Molly and Jonathan___ , Case No._____
                     Debtor   (If known)

SCHEDULE G—EXECUTORY CONTRACTS AND UNEXPIRED LEASES

Describe all executory contracts of any nature and all unexpired leases of real personal property. Include any timeshare interests.

State nature of debtor's interest in contract, i.e., "Purchaser," "Agent," etc. State whether debtor is the lessor or lessee of a lease.

Provide the names and complete mailing addresses of all other parties to each lease or contract described.

NOTE: A party listed on this schedule will not receive notice of the filing of this case unless the party is also scheduled in the appropriate schedule of creditors.

☐ Check this box if debtor has no executory contracts or unexpired leases.

NAME AND MAILING ADDRESS, INCLUDING ZIP CODE, OF OTHER PARTIES TO LEASE OR CONTRACT	DESCRIPTION OF CONTRACT OR LEASE AND NATURE OF DEBTOR'S INTEREST. STATE WHETHER LEASE IS FOR NONRESIDENTIAL REAL PROPERTY. STATE CONTRACT NUMBER OF ANY GOVERNMENT CONTRACT
Scarborough Road South Homeowners Association 1 Scarborough Road South Cleveland Hts, OH 41118	Homeowner's Association Contract for residential property, signed 10/XX, expires 12/XX. Provides for maintenance, gardening and repairs of property.

In re ___Maytag, Molly and Jonathan___,   Case No._____

Debtor   (If known)

SCHEDULE H—CODEBTORS

Provide the information requested concerning any person or entity, other than a spouse in a joint case, that is also liable on any debts listed by debtor in the schedules of creditors. Include all guarantors and co-signers. In community property states, a married debtor not filing a joint case should report the name and address of the nondebtor spouse on this schedule. Include all names used by the nondebtor spouse during the six years immediately preceding the commencement of this case.

☐ Check this box if debtor has no codebtors.

NAME AND ADDRESS OF CODEBTOR	NAME AND ADDRESS OF CREDITOR
Bonnie Johnson 40 Mayfield University Hts, OH 44118	Fanny's Furniture 14–4th Street Cleveland, OH 44114

In re ___Maytag, Molly and Jonathan___ ,   Case No._____
                    Debtor   (If known)

SCHEDULE I—CURRENT INCOME OF INDIVIDUAL DEBTOR(S)

The column labled "Spouse" must be completed in all cases filed by joint debtors and by a married debtor in a Chapter 12 or 13 case whether or not a joint petition is filed, unless the spouses are separated and a joint petition is not filed.

DEBTOR'S MARITAL STATUS:	DEPENDENTS OF DEBTOR AND SPOUSE		
	NAMES	AGE	RELATIONSHIP
Married	Sara Maytag	14	daughter
	Harold Maytag	12	son

Employment:	DEBTOR	SPOUSE
Occupation	Clerk/typist	Construction Worker
Name of Employer	Typing Circles	Cleveland Builder
How long employed	1 1/2 years	4 years
Address of Employer	40 Euclid Drive Cleveland, OH 44112	100 Chester Way Cleveland, OH 44114

INCOME: (Estimate of average monthly income)	DEBTOR	SPOUSE
Current monthly gross wages, salary, and commissions (pro rate if not paid monthly)	$ 1,450	$ 3,000
Estimated monthly overtime	$ 0	$ 0
SUBTOTAL	$ 1,450	$ 3,000
LESS PAYROLL DEDUCTIONS		
a. Payroll taxes and Social Security	$ 350	$ 600
b. Insurance	$ N/A	$ 250
c. Union dues	$ N/A	$ 50
d. Other (Specify: _____)	$ N/A	$ N/A
SUBTOTAL OF PAYROLL DEDUCTIONS	$ 350	$ 900
TOTAL NET MONTHLY TAKE HOME PAY	$ 1,100	$ 2,100
Regular income from operation of business or profession or farm (attach detailed statement)	$ N/A	$ N/A
Income from real property	$ N/A	$ N/A
Interest and dividends	$ 100	$ 100
Alimony, maintenance or support payments payable to the debtor for the debtor's use or that of dependents listed above	$ N/A	$ N/A
Social Security or other government assistance		
(Specify:_____)	$ N/A	$ N/A
Pension or retirement income	$ N/A	$ N/A
Other monthly income	$ N/A	$ N/A
(Specify:_____)	$ N/A	$ N/A
_____	$ N/A	$ N/A
TOTAL MONTHLY INCOME	$ 1,200	$ 2,200

TOTAL COMBINED MONTHLY INCOME $3,400 _____   (Report also on Summary of Schedules)

Describe any increase or decrease of more than 10% in any of the above categories anticipated to occur within the year following the filing of this document:

N/A

In re ___Maytag, Molly and Jonathan___,   Case No._____
                    Debtor   (If known)

SCHEDULE J—CURRENT EXPENDITURES OF INDIVIDUAL DEBTOR(S)

Complete this schedule by estimating the average monthly expenses of the debtor and the debtor's family. Pro rate any payments made bi-weekly, quarterly, semi-annually, or annually to show monthly rate.

☐ Check this box if a joint petition is filed and debtor's spouse maintains a separate household. Complete a separate schedule of expenditures labeled "Spouse."

Rent or home mortgage payment (include lot rented for mobile home)	$	650
Are real estate taxes included? Yes _X_ No _____		
Is property insurance included? Yes _X_ No _____		
Utilities: Electricity and heating fuel	$	245
Water and sewer	$	40
Telephone	$	85
Other _____garbage_____	$	15
Home maintenance (repairs and upkeep)	$	175
Food	$	550
Clothing	$	125
Laundry and dry cleaning	$	50
Medical and dental expenses	$	400
Transportation (not including car payments)	$	80
Recreation, clubs and entertainment, newspapers, magazines, etc.	$	30
Charitable contributions	$	50
Insurance (not deducted from wages or included in home mortgage payments)		
Homeowner's or renter's	$	120
Life	$	N/A
Health	$	N/A
Auto	$	60
Other _____	$	N/A
Taxes (not deducted from wages or included in home mortgage payments)		
(Specify: ___income taxes to IRS & Ohio Dept. of Tax___)	$	200
Installment payments: (In Chapter 12 and 13 cases, do not list payments to be included in the plan)		
Auto	$	N/A
Other _____credit card accounts_____	$	400
Other _____loans_____	$	550
Alimony, maintenance, and support paid to others	$	600
Payments for support of additional dependents not living at your home	$	N/A
Regular expenses from operation of business, profession, or farm (attach detailed statement)	$	N/A
Other _____	$	N/A
TOTAL MONTHLY EXPENSES (Report also on Summary of Schedules)	$	4,425

[FOR CHAPTER 12 AND CHAPTER 13 DEBTORS ONLY]
Provide the information requested below, including whether plan payments are to be made bi-weekly, monthly, annually, or at some other regular interval.

A. Total projected monthly income N/A	$	_____
B. Total projected monthly expenses	$	_____
C. Excess income (A minus B)	$	_____
D. Total amount to be paid into plan each _____	$	_____
(interval)		

United States Bankruptcy Court

Northern _____ District of ___ Ohio, Eastern Division ___

In re ___ Maytag, Molly and Jonathan ___,   Case No._____
        Debtor   (If known)

SUMMARY OF SCHEDULES

Indicate as to each schedule whether that schedule is attached and state the number of pages in each. Report the totals from Schedules A, B, D, E, F, I and J in the boxes provided. Add the amounts from Schedules A and B to determine the total amount of the debtor's assets. Add the amounts from Schedules D, E and F to determine the total amount of the debtor's liabilities.

NAME OF SCHEDULE		ATTACHED (YES/NO)	NUMBER OF SHEETS	AMOUNTS SCHEDULED		
				ASSETS	LIABILITIES	OTHER
A	Real Property	Yes	1	$ 100,000		
B	Personal Property	Yes	4	$ 29,692		
C	Property Claimed as Exempt	Yes	2			
D	Creditors Holding Secured Claims	Yes	2		$ 92,200	
E	Creditors Holding Unsecured Priority Claims	Yes	2		$ 3,000	
F	Creditors Holding Unsecured Nonpriority Claims	Yes	3		$ 52,450	
G	Executory Contracts and Unexpired Leases	Yes	1			
H	Codebtors	Yes	1			
I	Current Income of Individual Debtor(s)	Yes	1			$ 3,400
J	Current Expenditures of Individual Debtor(s)	Yes	1			$ 4,425
Total Number of Sheets of All Schedules ➡			18			
Total Assets ➡				$ 129,692		
Total Liabilities ➡					$ 147,650	

In re ___Maytag, Molly and Jonathan___,   Case No._____

Debtor   (If known)

DECLARATION CONCERNING DEBTOR'S SCHEDULES

DECLARATION UNDER PENALTY OF PERJURY BY INDIVIDUAL DEBTOR

I declare under penalty of perjury that I have read the foregoing summary and schedules consisting of ____**19**____
sheets, and that they are true and correct to the best of my knowledge, information, and belief.   (Total shown on summary page plus 1)

Date___July 3, 20XX___   Signature___*Molly Maytag*___

Debtor

Date___July 3, 20XX___   Signature___*Jonathan Maytag*___

(Joint Debtor, if any)

[If joint case, both spouses must sign.]

CERTIFICATION AND SIGNATURE OF NON-ATTORNEY BANKRUPTCY PETITION PREPARER (See 11 U.S.C. § 110)

I certify that I am a bankruptcy petition preparer as defined in 11 U.S.C. § 110, that I prepared this document for compensation, and that I have provided the debtor with a copy of this document.

____N/A____   _____

Printed or Typed Name of Bankruptcy Petition Preparer   Social Security No.

_____   _____

Address

Names and Social Security numbers of all other individuals who prepared or assisted in preparing this document:

If more than one person prepared this document, attach additional signed sheets conforming to the appropriate Official Form for each person.

X_____   _____

Signature of Bankruptcy Petition Preparer   Date

A bankruptcy petition preparer's failure to comply with the provisions of Title 11 and the Federal Rules of Bankruptcy Procedure may result in fine or imprisonment or both. 11 U.S.C. § 110; 18 U.S.C. § 156.

DECLARATION UNDER PENALTY OF PERJURY ON BEHALF OF CORPORATION OR PARTNERSHIP

I, the _____**N/A**_____ [the president or other officer or an authorized agent of the corporation or a member or an authorized agent of the partnership] of the _____ [corporation or partnership] named as debtor in this case, declare under penalty of perjury that I have read the foregoing summary and schedules, consisting of _____ sheets, and that they are true and correct to the best of my knowledge, information, and belief.

(Total shown on summary page plus 1)

Date_____   Signature_____

_____

[Print or type name of individual signing on behalf of debtor]

[An individual signing on behalf of a partnership or corporation must indicate position or relationship to debtor.]

Penalty for making a false statement or concealing property: Fine of up to $500,000, imprisonment for up to 5 years, or both. 18 U.S.C. §§ 152 and 3571.

FORM 7. STATEMENT OF FINANCIAL AFFAIRS

UNITED STATES BANKRUPTCY COURT

__Northern__ DISTRICT OF Ohio, Eastern Division

In re: __Maytag, Molly and Jonathan__ ,   Case No. _____
(Name)   (If known)

Debtor

STATEMENT OF FINANCIAL AFFAIRS

This statement is to be completed by every debtor. Spouses filing a joint petition may file a single statement on which the information for both spouses is combined. If the case is filed under Chapter 12 or Chapter 13, a married debtor must furnish information for both spouses whether or not a joint petition is filed, unless the spouses are separated and a joint petition is not filed. An individual debtor engaged in business as a sole proprietor, partner, family farmer, or self-employed professional, should provide the information requested on this statement concerning all such activities as well as the individual's personal affairs.

Questions 1–15 are to be completed by all debtors. Debtors that are or have been in business, as defined below, also must complete Questions 16–21. **Each question must be answered. If the answer to any question is "None," or the question is not applicable, mark the box labeled "None."** If additional space is needed for the answer to any question, use and attach a separate sheet properly identified with the case name, case number (if known), and the number of the question.

DEFINITIONS

"In business." A debtor is "in business" for the purpose of this form if the debtor is a corporation or partnership. An individual debtor is "in business" for the purpose of this form if the debtor is or has been, within the two years immediately preceding the filing of this bankruptcy case, any of the following: an officer, director, managing executive, or person in control of a corporation; a partner, other than a limited partner, of a partnership; a sole proprietor or self-employed.

"Insider." The term "insider" includes but is not limited to: relatives of the debtor; general partners of the debtor and their relatives; corporations of which the debtor is an officer, director, or person in control; officers, directors, and any person in control of a corporate debtor and their relatives; affiliates of the debtor and insiders of such affiliates; any managing agent of the debtor. 11 U.S.C. § 101(30).

1. **Income from employment or operation of business**

None ☐   State the gross amount of income the debtor has received from employment, trade, or profession, or from operation of the debtor's business from the beginning of this calendar year to the date this case was commenced. State also the gross amounts received during the **two years** immediately preceding this calendar year. (A debtor that maintains, or has maintained, financial records on the basis of a fiscal rather than a calendar year may report fiscal year income. Identify the beginning and ending dates of the debtor's fiscal year.) If a joint petition is filed, state income for each spouse separately. (Married debtors filing under Chapter 12 or Chapter 13 must state income of both spouses whether or not a joint petition is filed, unless the spouses are separated and a joint petition is not filed.)

AMOUNT		SOURCE (If more than one)
$6,000	(1/1/XX–7/3/XX)	Wife's employment
$18,000	(1/1/XX–7/3/XX)	Husband's employment
$14,000	(19XY)	Wife's employment
$29,000	(19XY)	Husband's employment
$11,000	(19XZ)	Wife's employment
$16,000	(19XZ)	Husband's employment

2. Income other than from employment or operation of business

None ☐ State the amount of income received by the debtor other than from employment, trade, profession, or operation of the debtor's business during the **two years** immediately preceding the commencement of this case. Give particulars. If a joint petition is filed, state income for each spouse separately. (Married debtors filing under Chapter 12 or Chapter 13 must state income for each spouse whether or not a joint petition is filed, unless the spouses are separated and a joint petition is not filed.)

AMOUNT	SOURCE
$300	20XX, stock dividends (J)
$740	20XY, stock dividends (J)
$4,000	20XX, worker's comp benefits (H)

3. Payments to creditors

None ☐ a. List all payments on loans, installment purchases of goods or services, and other debts, aggregating more than $600 to any creditor, made within **90 days** immediately preceding the commencement of this case. (Married debtors filing under Chapter 12 or Chapter 13 must include payments by either or both spouses whether or not a joint petition is not filed.)

NAME AND ADDRESS OF CREDITOR	DATES OF PAYMENTS	AMOUNT PAID	AMOUNT STILL OWING
Ameritrust	4/17/XX	$650	$87,000
10 Financial Way	5/17/XX	$650	
Cleveland Hts, OH 44118	6/17/XX	$650	

None ☐ b. List all payments made within **one year** immediately preceding the commencement of this case, to or for the benefit of, creditors who are or were insiders. (Married debtors filing under Chapter 12 or Chapter 13 must include payments by either or both spouses whether or not a joint petition is filed, unless the spouses are separated and a joint petition is not filed.)

NAME AND ADDRESS OF CREDITOR; RELATIONSHIP TO DEBTOR	DATES OF PAYMENTS	AMOUNT PAID	AMOUNT STILL OWING
Ellen Rogers 900 Grand View Jackson, WY 83001 (ex-wife, mother of husband's 2 children)	8/XX to 5/XY	$600/month	$600/month since 6/XY

4. Suits, executions, garnishments and attachments

None ☐ a. List all suits to which the debtor is or was a party within **one year** immediately preceding the filing of this bankruptcy case. (Married debtors filing under Chapter 12 or Chapter 13 must include information concerning either or both spouses whether or not a joint petition is filed, unless the spouses are separated and a joint petition is not filed.)

CAPTION OF SUIT AND CASE NUMBER	NATURE OF PROCEEDING	COURT AND LOCATION	STATUS OR DISPOSITION
Cleveland Hospital v. Jonathan Maytag (H)	Suit for doctor's fee and medical bills	Cleveland Municipal Ct., Cleveland, OH	trial set 9/7/XX
Dennis Dentist v. Molly M. Maytag, #91-8080 (W)	Suit for dentist's fees	Cleveland Hts Small Claims Court, Cleveland, OH	open
Freedom Financial v. Jonathan & Molly Maytag #90-9101 (J)	Suit for unpaid American Express bill	Cleveland Municipal Ct., Cleveland, OH	open
American Allowance v. Jonathan & Molly Maytag #90-7400 (J)	Suit for unpaid VISA bill	Cleveland Municipal Ct., Cleveland, OH	open

None b. Describe all property that has been attached, garnished or seized under any legal or equitable process within **one year** immediately
☐   preceding the commencement of this case. (Married debtors filing under Chapter 12 or Chapter 13 must include information
       concerning property of either or both spouses whether or not a joint petition is filed, unless the spouses are separated and a joint petition
       is not filed.)

NAME AND ADDRESS OF PERSON FOR WHOSE BENEFIT PROPERTY WAS SEIZED	DATE OF SEIZURE	DESCRIPTION AND VALUE OF PROPERTY
Quality Collection Agency 21 Main Street Cleveland, OH 44115	on or about 2/XX	(J) bank account levy – $650
Quality Collection Agency 21 Main Street Cleveland, OH 44115	4/10/XX to 6/30/XX	(H) wage garnishment - $850

5. Repossessions, foreclosures and returns

None   List all property that has been repossessed by a creditor, sold at a foreclosure sale, transferred through a deed in lieu of foreclosure or
☐   returned to the seller within **one year** immediately preceding the commencement of this case. (Married debtors filing under Chapter 12 or
       Chapter 13 must include information concerning property of either or both spouses whether or not a joint petition is filed, unless the spouses
       are separated and a joint petition is not filed.)

NAME AND ADDRESS OF CREDITOR OR SELLER	DATE OF REPOSSESSION, FORECLOSURE SALE, TRANSFER OR RETURN	DESCRIPTION AND VALUE OF PROPERTY
Ameritrust 10 Financial Way Cleveland Hts, OH 44118	6/18/XX repossessed	(J) 1993 Honda Civic, approximate value $4,500
Shaker Savings 44 Trust St. Cleveland Hts, OH 44118	6/30/XX repossessed	(J) 1985 Buick Skylark, approximate value $3,000

6. Assignments and receiverships

None a. Describe any assignment of property for the benefit of creditors made within **120 days** immediately preceding the commencement of
☒   this case. (Married debtors filing under Chapter 12 or Chapter 13 must include any assignment by either or both spouses whether or not
       a joint petition is filed, unless the spouses are separated and a joint petition is not filed.)

NAME AND ADDRESS OF ASSIGNEE	DATE OF ASSIGNMENT	TERMS OF ASSIGNMENT OR SETTLEMENT

None b. List all property which has been in the hands of a custodian, receiver, or court-appointed official within **one year** immediately preceding
[X]   the commencement of this case. (Married debtors filing under Chapter 12 or Chapter 13 must include information concerning property
         of either or both spouses whether or not a joint petition is filed, unless the spouses are separated and a joint petition is not filed.)

NAME AND ADDRESS OF CUSTODIAN	NAME AND LOCATION OF COURT; CASE TITLE & NUMBER	DATE OF ORDER	DESCRIPTION AND VALUE OF PROPERTY

7. Gifts

None   List all gifts or charitable contributions made within **one year** immediately preceding the commencement of this case except ordinary
[X]   and usual gifts to family members aggregating less than $200 in value per individual family member and charitable contributions aggregating
         less than $100 per recipient. (Married debtors filing under Chapter 12 or Chapter 13 must include gifts or contributions by either or both
         spouses whether or not a joint petition is filed, unless the spouses are separated and a joint petition is not filed.)

NAME AND ADDRESS OF PERSON OR ORGANIZATION	RELATIONSHIP TO DEBTOR, IF ANY	DATE OF GIFT	DESCRIPTION AND VALUE OF GIFT

8. Losses

None   List all losses from fire, theft, other casualty or gambling within **one year** immediately preceding the commencement of this case **or since
[ ]   the commencement of this case.** (Married debtors filing under Chapter 12 or Chapter 13 must include losses by either or both spouses
         whether or not a joint petition is filed, unless the spouses are separated and a joint petition is not filed.)

DESCRIPTION AND VALUE OF PROPERTY	DESCRIPTION OF CIRCUMSTANCES AND, IF LOSS WAS COVERED IN WHOLE OR IN PART BY INSURANCE, GIVE PARTICULARS	DATE OF LOSS
Mountain bike; $165	Daughter Sara's bicycle was stolen. Insurance covered replacement. We purchased new bike on 12/17/XY.	10/5/XX

9.　Payments related to debt counseling or bankruptcy

None
☐

List all payments made or property transferred by or on behalf of the debtor to any person, including attorneys, for consultation concerning debt consolidation, relief under the bankruptcy law or preparation of a petition in bankruptcy within **one year** immediately preceding the commencement of this case.

NAME AND ADDRESS OF PAYEE	DATE OF PAYMENT; NAME OF PAYOR IF OTHER THAN DEBTOR	AMOUNT OF MONEY OR DESCRIPTION AND VALUE OF PROPERTY
John White, Esq. 21 Main St. Cleveland, OH 44114	2/11/XX	(J)　$500 retainer fee paid

10.　Other transfers

None
☒

a.　List all other property, other than property transferred in the ordinary course of the business or financial affairs of the debtor, transferred either absolutely or as security within **one year** immediately preceding the commencement of this case. (Married debtors filing under Chapter 12 or Chapter 13 must include transfers by either or both spouses whether or not a joint petition is filed, unless the spouses are separated and a joint petition is not filed.)

NAME AND ADDRESS OF TRANSFEREE; RELATIONSHIP TO DEBTOR	DATE	DESCRIBE PROPERTY TRANSFERRED AND VALUE RECEIVED

11.　Closed financial accounts

None
☐

List all financial accounts and instruments held in the name of the debtor or for the benefit of the debtor which were closed, sold, or otherwise transferred within **one year** immediately preceding the commencement of this case. Include checking, savings, or other financial accounts, certificates of deposit, or other instruments; shares and share accounts held in banks, credit unions, pension funds, cooperatives, associations, brokerage houses and other financial institutions. (Married debtors filing under Chapter 12 or Chapter 13 must include information concerning accounts or instruments held by or for either or both spouses whether or not a joint petition is filed, unless the spouses are separated and a joint petition is not filed.)

NAME AND ADDRESS OF INSTITUTION	TYPE AND NUMBER OF ACCOUNT AND AMOUNT OF FINAL BALANCE	AMOUNT AND DATE OF SALE OR CLOSING
Ohio Savings 1818 Lakeshore Avenue Cleveland, OH 44123	(H)　Checking account #058-118061 final balance $84.12	12/2/XY

12. Safe deposit boxes

None ☐

List each safe deposit or other box or depository in which the debtor has or had securities, cash, or other valuables within **one year** immediately preceding the commencement of this case. (Married debtors filing under Chapter 12 or Chapter 13 must include boxes or depositories of either or both spouses whether or not a joint petition is filed, unless the spouses are separated and a joint petition is not filed.)

NAME AND ADDRESS OF BANK OR OTHER DEPOSITORY	NAMES AND ADDRESSES OF THOSE WITH ACCESS TO BOX OR DEPOSITORY	DESCRIPTION OF CONTENTS	DATE OF TRANSFER OR SURRENDER, IF ANY
Ameritrust 10 Financial Way Cleveland Hts., OH 44118	Molly Maytag Jonathan Maytag 21 Scarborough Rd. So. Cleveland Hts, OH 41118	stock certificates for Trusso Corp., Investco Ltd., and Rayco Co.	N/A

13. Setoffs

None ☒

List all setoffs made by any creditor, including a bank, against a debt or deposit of the debtor within **90 days** preceding the commencement of this case. (Married debtors filing under Chapter 12 or Chapter 13 must include information concerning either or both spouses whether or not a joint petition is filed, unless the spouses are separated and a joint petition is not filed.)

NAME AND ADDRESS OF CREDITOR	DATE OF SETOFF	AMOUNT OF SETOFF

14. Property held for another person

None ☐

List all property owned by another person that the debtor holds or controls.

NAME AND ADDRESS OF OWNER	DESCRIPTION AND VALUE OF PROPERTY	LOCATION OF PROPERTY
Paul & Bonnie Johnson 40 Mayfield University Hts, OH 44118	Poodle – Binkie $100	residence
Felicia Maytag 8 Superior Rd Cleveland, OH 44114	19XW Ford Pickup $750	residence

15. Prior address of debtor

None ☒

If the debtor has moved within the **two years** immediately preceding the commencement of this case, list all premises which the debtor occupied during that period and vacated prior to the commencement of this case. If a joint petition is filed, report also any separate address of either spouse.

ADDRESS	NAME USED	DATES OF OCCUPANCY

The following questions are to be completed by every debtor that is a corporation or partnership and by any individual debtor who is or has been, within the **two years** immediately preceding the commencement of this case, any of the following: an officer, director, managing executive, or owner of more than 5 percent of the voting securities of a corporation; a partner, other than a limited partner, of a partnership; a sole proprietor or otherwise self-employed.

*(An individual or joint debtor should complete this portion of the statement **only** if the debtor is or has been in business, as defined above, within the two years immediately preceding the commencement of this case.)*

N/A

16. Nature, location and name of business

None a. If the debtor is an individual, list the names and addresses of all businesses in which the debtor was an officer, director, partner, or
☐ managing executive of a corporation, partnership, sole proprietorship, or was a self-employed professional within the **two years** immediately preceding the commencement of this case, or in which the debtor owned 5 percent or more of the voting or equity securities, within the **two years** immediately preceding the commencement of this case.

b. If the debtor is a partnership, list the names and addresses of all businesses in which the debtor was a partner or owned 5 percent or more of the voting securities, within the **two years** immediately preceding the commencement of this case.

c. If the debtor is a corporation, list the names and addresses of all businesses in which the debtor was a partner or owned 5 percent or more of the voting securities, within the **two years** immediately preceding the commencement of this case.

NAME	ADDRESS	NATURE OF BUSINESS	BEGINNING AND ENDING DATES OF OPERATION

17. Books, records and financial statements

None a. List all bookkeepers and accountants who within the **six years** immediately preceding the filing of this bankruptcy case kept or
☐ supervised the keeping of books of account and records of the debtor.

NAME AND ADDRESS	DATES SERVICES RENDERED

None b. List all firms or individuals who within the **two years** immediately preceding the filing of this bankruptcy case have audited the books of
☐ account and records, or prepared a financial statement of the debtor.

NAME AND ADDRESS	DATES SERVICES RENDERED

None ☐ c. List all firms or individuals who at the time of the commencement of this case were in possession of the books of account and records of the debtor. If any of the books of account and records are not available, explain.

NAME   ADDRESS

None ☐ d. List all financial institutions, creditors and other parties, including mercantile and trade agencies, to whom a financial statement was issued within the **two years** immediately preceding the commencement of this case by the debtor.

NAME AND ADDRESS   DATE ISSUED

18. Inventories

None ☐ a. List the dates of the last two inventories taken of your property, the name of the person who supervised the taking of each inventory, and the dollar amount and basis of each inventory.

DATE OF INVENTORY   INVENTORY SUPERVISOR   DOLLAR AMOUNT OF INVENTORY
                                                         (Specify cost, market or other basis)

None ☐ b. List the name and address of the person having possession of the records of each of the two inventories reported in a., above.

DATE OF INVENTORY   NAME AND ADDRESSES OF
                                               CUSTODIAN OF INVENTORY RECORDS

19. Current partners, officers, directors and shareholders

None ☐ a. If the debtor is a partnership, list the nature and percentage of partnership interest of each member of the partnership.

NAME AND ADDRESS   NATURE OF INTEREST   PERCENTAGE OF INTEREST

None b. If the debtor is a corporation, list all officers and directors of the corporation, and each stockholder who directly or indirectly owns, controls, or holds 5 percent or more of the voting securities of the corporation.

NAME AND ADDRESS	TITLE	NATURE AND PERCENTAGE OF STOCK OWNERSHIP

20. Former partners, officers, directors and shareholders

None a. If the debtor is a partnership, list each member who withdrew from the partnership within **one year** immediately preceding the commencement of this case.

NAME	ADDRESS	DATE OF WITHDRAWAL

None b. If the debtor is a corporation, list all officers or directors whose relationship with the corporation terminated within **one year** immediately preceding the commencement of this case.

NAME AND ADDRESS	TITLE	DATE OF TERMINATION

21. Withdrawals from a partnership or distributions by a corporation

None If the debtor is a partnership or corporation, list all withdrawals or distributions credited or given to an insider, including compensation in any form, bonuses, loans, stock redemptions, options exercised and any other perquisite during **one year** immediately preceding the commencement of this case

NAME AND ADDRESS OF RECIPIENT; RELATIONSHIP TO DEBTOR	DATE AND PURPOSE OF WITHDRAWAL	AMOUNT OF MONEY OR DESCRIPTION AND VALUE OF PROPERTY

[If completed by an individual or individual and spouse]

I declare under penalty of perjury that I have read the answers contained in the foregoing statement of financial affairs and any attachments thereto and that they are true and correct.

Date ____July 3, 20XX____   Signature of Debtor _____*Molly Maytag*_____

Date ____July 3, 20XX____   Signature of Joint Debtor (if any) _____*Jonathan Maytag*_____

CERTIFICATION AND SIGNATURE OF NON-ATTORNEY BANKRUPTCY PETITION PREPARER (See 11 U.S.C. § 110)

I certify that I am a bankruptcy petition preparer as defined in 11 U.S.C. § 110, that I prepared this document for compensation, and that I have provided the debtor with a copy of this document.

N/A

_____   _____
Printed or Typed Name of Bankruptcy Petition Preparer   Social Security No.

_____

_____
Address

Names and Social Security numbers of all other individuals who prepared or assisted in preparing this document:

If more than one person prepared this document, attach additional signed sheets conforming to the appropriate Official Form for each person.

X _____   _____
Signature of Bankruptcy Petition Preparer   Date

A bankruptcy petition preparer's failure to comply with the provisions of title 11 and the Federal Rules of Bankruptcy Procedure may result in fine or imprisonment or both. 11 U.S.C. § 110; 18 U.S.C. § 156.

[If completed by or on behalf of a partnership or corporation]   N/A

I declare under penalty of perjury that I have read the answers contained in the foregoing statement of financial affairs and any attachments thereto and that they are true and correct to the best of my knowledge, information and belief.

Date _____   Signature _____

_____
Print Name and Title

[An individual signing on behalf of a partnership or corporation must indicate position or relationship to debtor.]

____0____ *continuation sheets attached*

Penalty for presenting fraudulent claim: Fine of up to $500,000 or imprisonment for up to 5 years, or both. 18 U.S.C. §§ 152 and 3571.

Form 8. CHAPTER 7 INDIVIDUAL DEBTOR'S STATEMENT OF INTENTION

UNITED STATES BANKRUPTCY COURT

_____Northern_____ DISTRICT OF __Ohio, Eastern Division__

In re __Maytag, Molly and Jonathan__ ,   Case No. _____
                 (Name)   (If known)

                      Debtor   Chapter _____7_____

1. I have filed a schedule of assets and liabilities which includes consumer debts secured by property of the estate.

2. I intend to do the following with respect to the property of the estate which secures those consumer debts:

   a. *Property to be surrendered.*

	Description of Property	Creditor's Name
1.	N/A	
2.		
3.		

   b. *Property to be retained.*   [*Check any applicable statement.*]

	Description of property	Creditor's name	Property is claimed as exempt	Property will be redeemed pursuant to 11 U.S.C. § 722	Debt will be reaffirmed pursuant to 11 USC § 524(c)
1.	Residence	Ameritrust (mortgage)	X		
2.	Ameritrust (2nd mortgage)		X		
3.	Ohio Savings (judgment lien)				X
4.	Computer	Computers for Sale		X	
5.	Bedroom furniture	Fanny's Furniture		X	

Date: __July 3, 20XX__   *Molly Maytag/Jonathan Maytag*
                                      Signature of Debtor

CERTIFICATION OF NON-ATTORNEY BANKRUPTCY PETITION PREPARER (See 11 U.S.C. § 110)

   I certify that I am a bankruptcy petition preparer as defined in 11 U.S.C. § 110, that I prepared this document for compensation, and that I have provided the debtor with a copy of this document.

   N/A

Printed or Typed Name of Bankruptcy Petition Preparer   Social Security No.

Address

Names and Social Security numbers of all other individuals who prepared or assisted in preparing this document:

If more than one person prepared this document, attach additional signed sheets conforming to the appropriate Official Form for each person.

X

Signature of Bankruptcy Petition Preparer   Date

A bankruptcy petition preparer's failure to comply with the provisions of title 11 and the Federal Rules of Bankruptcy Procedure may result in fine or imprisonment or both. 11 U.S.C. § 110; 18 U.S.C. § 156.

26% PLAN

(ATTORNEY NAME:) ___not applicable___

(ADDRESS:) _____

(CITY) _____ (STATE:) _____

(ZIP:) _____

(PHONE NUMBER:) (____) _____

(BAR NUMBER:) __Debtors Pro Se__

DEBTORS: __Martin and Ellen Herchoo__   CASE NO.: _____

DEBTORS PRELIMINARY CHAPTER 13 PLAN

DATE OF PLAN __2/23/XX__   FIRST PAYMENT DUE TO TRUSTEE __3/25/XX__

INCOME $ __6,110__ TRUSTEE PAYMENTS $ __1,800__ FOR _36_ MONTHS PLAN BASE AMOUNT $ _____

EXPENSES $ __4,310__ $ _____ FOR ____ MONTHS UNSECURED % __26__

SURPLUS $ __1,800__ $ _____ FOR ____ MONTHS

ADMINISTRATIVE   NOTICING FEES: # _____ + 3 X 3 X .79 = $ _____

            ATTORNEY FEES: TOTAL _____ THRU PLAN _____

HOME MORTGAGE   Regular payments beginning __3/1/XX__ to be paid direct. Arrearages to be paid by Trustee as follows:

	ARREARS	THRU	%	TERM	PAYMENT
1ST LIEN __Big Home Loan Bank__	$ __10,800__	_____	10	6 mos	$ __1,800__
2ND LIEN _____	$ _____				$ _____

SECURED CREDITORS	COLLATERAL	CLAIM	VALUE	%	TERM	PAYMENT
1. Car Finance Co.	20XX Nissan	$ __372__	$ __7,400__	8	1 mo.	$ __372__
2. _____	_____	$ _____	$ _____	___	_____	$ _____
3. _____	_____	$ _____	$ _____	___	_____	$ _____
4. _____	_____	$ _____	$ _____	___	_____	$ _____
5. _____	_____	$ _____	$ _____	___	_____	$ _____

ANY DEFICIENCY WILL AUTOMATICALLY BE "SPLIT" AND INCLUDED IN UNSECURED.

PRIORITY CREDITORS	TYPE	DISPUTED AMOUNT	CLAIM	TERM	PAYMENT
1. IRS	tax	$ _____	$ __33,762__	19 mos.	$ __1,800__
2. _____		$ _____	$ _____		$ _____

SPECIAL CLASS		BASIS	AMOUNT	TERM	PAYMENT
1. River Bank	codebtor		$ __3,918__	2+ mos.	$ __1,800__
2. Sweeter's Bank	codebtor		$ __1,411__	1 mo.	$ __1,411__

UNSECURED CREDITORS	CLAIM		CREDITORS	CLAIM		CREDITORS	CLAIM
1. Summer Vacations Co.	$ 8,880	6.		$ _____	11.		$ _____
2. Visa	$ __12,789__	7.		$ _____	12.		$ _____
3. MasterCard	$ __6,452__	8.		$ _____	13.		$ _____
4. Ken Williams	$ __1,215__	9.		$ _____	14.		$ _____
5. _____	$ _____	10.		$ _____	15.		$ _____

TOTAL UNSECURED AND DEFICIENCIES $ __29,336__

_X_ CHECK HERE IF ADDITIONAL INFORMATION APPEARS ON REVERSE SIDE (EXECUTORY CONTRACTS? MISCELLANEOUS?)

CERTIFICATE OF SERVICE

I certify that a copy of the above and foregoing "Debtor's Preliminary Chapter 13 Plan" and an "Authorization for Pre-Confirmation Disbursement" was by me on this __25th__ day __February__ of 20__XX__ served on the trustee and all creditors listed on the original matrix and any amended matrix filed in this case by United States First Class mail.

Martin Herchoo

Attorney for Debtor or Pro Se Debtor

SPECIAL PROVISIONS:

(Balloon, proceeds of sale;

recovery on lawsuit, etc.

1. We reject our leased time share with Summer Vacations Co.

2. We will file a Motion to avoid Ken William's judicial lien against our house.

3. We propose making our regular house and car payments, and our home equity loan payments ($335/month), outside the plan.

ADDITIONAL CREDITORS:

HOME MORTGAGE:

	ARREARS	THRU	%	TERM	PAYMENT
3RD LIEN _____ $_____		_____	____	_____	$_____
4TH LIEN _____ $_____		_____	____	_____	$_____

SECURED CREDITORS	COLLATERAL	CLAIM	VALUE	%	TERM	PAYMENT
6. _____	_____	$_____	$_____	____	_____	$_____
7. _____	_____	$_____	$_____	____	_____	$_____
8. _____	_____	$_____	$_____	____	_____	$_____
9. _____	_____	$_____	$_____	____	_____	$_____
10. _____	_____	$_____	$_____	____	_____	$_____

PRIORITY CREDITORS	DISPUTED AMOUNT	CLAIM	TERM	PAYMENT
3. _____	$_____	$_____	_____	$_____
4. _____	$_____	$_____	_____	$_____

SPECIAL CLASS	BASIS	AMOUNT	TERM	PAYMENT
3. _____	_____	$_____	_____	$_____
4. _____	_____	$_____	_____	$_____

UNSECURED CREDITORS	CLAIM	CREDITORS	CLAIM	CREDITORS	CLAIM
_____	$_____	_____	$_____	_____	$_____
_____	$_____	_____	$_____	_____	$_____
_____	$_____	_____	$_____	_____	$_____
_____	$_____	_____	$_____	_____	$_____
_____	$_____	_____	$_____	_____	$_____

48% PLAN

DEBTOR(S)_____Martin and Ellen Herchoo_____   CASE NO. _____

CHAPTER 13 PLAN OR SUMMARY

I.   The projected disposable income of the debtor(s) is submitted to the supervision and control of the Trustee and the Debtor(s) shall pay to the Trustee the sum of:

$ _1,800_____   ☐ Weekly   ☐ Bi-weekly   ☐ Semi-monthly   ☒ Monthly

☒ Direct Payment   ☐ Payroll Deduction on Wages of: ☐ Debtor   ☐ Spouse

Length of plan is approximately ___40_____ months, and total debt to be paid through plan is approximately $_____70,445_____ .

II.   From the payments so received the Trustee shall make disbursements as follows:

A.   PRIORITY payments described in 11 USC §507 in full in deferred cash payments.

B.   The holder of each allowed SECURED claim shall retain the lien securing such claim until a discharge is granted and such claim shall be paid in full with interest at a rate of ___10___% per annum in deferred cash payments as follows:

    1.   Mortgage Debts:

Name of Mortgage company	Home-stead Yes/No	Total amount of debt	Arrears to be paid by Trustee	Months included in arrearage amount	Post-petition –OR– payments to begin Month/Year* (Direct to creditor)	Amount of regular mortgage to be paid by Trustee
Big Home Loan Bank	yes	239,715	10,800	10/XX–2/XX	3/XX	

    2.   Other Secured Debts:

Name of creditor	Total amount of debt	Debtor's value	Description collateral	If Applicable** Interest factor	Debtor's Fixed Payments
Car Finance Co.	8,250		19XX Nissan		355

C.   The Debtor(s) will make direct payments as follows:

Name of creditor	Total of debt	Description of collateral	Reason for direct payment
Car Finance Co.	8,250	19XX Nissan	only one month in arrears
Big Home Loan Bank	16,080	home	not in default (335/mo)

D.   Special provisions. Explanation:

1. We reject our leased homeshare with Summer Vacations Co.

2. We will give a Motion to Avoid Ken William's judicial lien against our house

3. Please pay 100% on unsecured debts with codebtors: Personal loan from River Bank; Personal loan from Sweeter's Bank

☒ This is an original plan.

☐ This is an amended plan replacing plan dated _____ .

☒ This plan proposes to pay unsecured creditors ___48___ %.

☒ Insurance on vehicle: ☒ Proof of Insurance attached, OR:

                    ☐ Insurance through Trustee requested

Dated: ___2/23/XX_____   *Martin Herchoo*
                                       Signature of Debtor

Dated: ___2/23/XX_____   *Ellen Herchoo*
                                       Signature of Debtor

100% PLAN

CHAPTER 13 PLAN

In Re: Martin and Ellen Herchoo   Dated: 2/23/XX _____

Debtor

In a joint case,
debtor means debtors in this plan.

Case No. _____

1. PAYMENTS BY DEBTOR —

    a. As of this date of this plan, the debtor has paid the trustee $ ___0_____ .

    b. After the date of this plan, the debtor will pay the trustee $ ___1,800___ per ___month___ for ___49___ months, beginning within 30 days after the filing of this plan for a total of $ ___88,200_____ .

    c. The debtor will also pay the trustee _____$1,203 in the 50th month_____

    d. The debtor will pay the trustee a total of $ _____89,403_____ [line 1(a) + line 1(b) + line 1(c)].

2. PAYMENTS BY TRUSTEE — The trustee will make payments only to creditors for which proofs of claim have been filed, make payments monthly as available, and collect the trustee's percentage fee of 10% for a total of $ ___8,940_____ [line 1 (d) x .10] or such lesser percentage as may be fixed by the Attorney General. For purposes of this plan, month one (1) is the month following the month in which the debtor makes the debtor's first payment. Unless ordered otherwise, the trustee will not make any payments until the plan is confirmed. Payments will accumulate and be paid following confirmation.

3. PRIORITY CLAIMS — The trustee shall pay in full all claims entitled to priority under § 507, including the following. The amounts listed are estimates only. The trustee will pay the amounts actually allowed.

Creditor	Estimated Claim	Monthly Payment	Beginning in Month #	Number of Payments	TOTAL PAYMENTS
a. Attorney Fees	$ _____	$ _____	_____	_____	$ _____
b. Internal Revenue Service	$ 33,762	$ 1,800	7	19	$ 33,762
c. State Dept. of Revenue	$ _____	$ _____	_____	_____	$ _____
d. _____	$ _____	$ _____	_____	_____	$ _____
e. TOTAL					$ 33,762

4. LONG-TERM SECURED CLAIMS NOT IN DEFAULT — The following creditor have secured claims. Payments are current and the debtor will continue to make all payments which come due after the date the petition was filed directly to the creditors. The creditors will retain their liens.

    a. Home equity loan through Big Home Loan Bank ($335 a month)

    b. _____

5. HOME MORTGAGES IN DEFAULT [§ 1322 (b)(5)] — The trustee will cure defaults (plus interest at the rate of 8 per cent per annum) on claims secured only by a security interest in real property that is the debtor's principal residence as follows. The debtor will maintain the regular payments which come due after the date the petition was filed. The creditors will retain their liens. The amounts of default are estimates only. The trustee will pay the actual amounts of default.

Creditor	Amount of Default	Monthly Payment	Beginning in Month #	Number of Payments	TOTAL PAYMENTS
a. Big Home Loan Bank	$ 10,800	$ 2,160	$ 1	$ 6	$ 10,800
b. _____	$ _____	$ _____	$ _____	$ _____	$ _____
c. _____	$ _____	$ _____	$ _____	$ _____	$ _____
d. TOTAL					$ 10,800

Chapter 13 Plan   Page 2

6. OTHER LONG-TERM SECURED CLAIMS IN DEFAULT [§ 1322 (b)(5)] — The trustee will cure defaults (plus interest at the rate of 8 per cent per annum) on other claims as follows and the debtor will maintain the regular payments which come due after the date the petition was filed. The creditors will retain their liens. The amounts of default are estimates only. The trustee will pay the actual amounts of default.

Creditor	Amount of Default	Monthly Payment	Beginning in Month #	Number of Payments	TOTAL PAYMENTS
a. Car Finance Co.	$ 372	$ 355	7	1	$ 372
b. _____	$_____	$_____	_____	_____	$_____
c. _____	$_____	$_____	_____	_____	$_____
d. TOTAL					$ 372

7. OTHER SECURED CLAIMS [§ 1325 (a)(5)] — The trustee will make payments to the following secured creditors having a value as of confirmation equal to the allowed amount of the creditor's secured claim using a discount rate of 8 percent. The creditor's allowed secured claim shall be the creditor's allowed claim or the value of the creditor's interest in the debtor's property, whichever is less. The creditors shall retain their liens. NOTE: NOTWITHSTANDING A CREDITOR'S PROOF OF CLAIM FILED BEFORE OR AFTER CONFIRMATION, THE AMOUNT LISTED IN THIS PARAGRAPH AS A CREDITOR'S SECURED CLAIM BINDS THE CREDITOR PURSUANT TO 11 U.S.C. § 1327 AND CONFIRMATION OF THE PLAN WILL BE CONSIDERED A DETERMINATION OF THE CREDITOR'S ALLOWED SECURED CLAIM UNDER 11 U.S.C. § 506 (a).

Creditor	Claim Amount	Secured Claim	Monthly Payment	Beginning in Month #	Number of Payments	TOTAL PAYMENTS
a. _____	$_____	$_____	$_____	_____	_____	$_____
b. _____	$_____	$_____	$_____	_____	_____	$_____
c. _____	$_____	$_____	$_____	_____	_____	$_____
d. TOTAL						$ 0

8. SEPARATE CLASS OF UNSECURED CREDITORS — In addition to the class of unsecured creditors specified in ¶ 9, there shall be a separate class of nonpriority unsecured creditors described as follows: __debts with codebtors__

   a. The debtor estimates that the total claims in this class are $ __5,329__ .

   b. The trustee will pay this class $ __5,329__ .

9. TIMELY FILED UNSECURED CREDITORS — The trustee will pay holders of nonpriority unsecured claims for which proofs of claim were timely filed the balance of all payments received by the trustee and not paid under ¶ 2, 3, 5, 6, 7 and 8 their pro rata share of approximately $ __29,336__ [line 1(d) minus lines 2, 3(e), 5(d), 6(d), 7(d) and 8 (b)].

   a. The debtor estimates that the total unsecured claims held by creditors listed in ¶ 7 are $ __0__

   b. The debtor estimates that the debtor's total unsecured claims (excluding those in ¶ 7 and ¶ 8) are $ __29,336__ .

   c. Total estimated unsecured claims are $ __29,336__ [line 9(a) + line 9(b)].

10. TARDILY-FILED UNSECURED CREDITORS — All money paid by the debtor to the trustee under ¶ 1, but not distributed by the trustee under ¶ 2, 3, 5, 6, 7, 8 or 9 shall be paid to holders of nonpriority unsecured claims for which proofs of claim were tardily filed.

11. OTHER PROVISIONS —
   1. We reject our leased timeshare with Summer Vacations Co.
   2. We will file a motion to avoid Ken William's judicial lien against our house.
   3. We propose making our regular house and car payments outside the plan.

12. SUMMARY PAYMENTS —

Trustee's Fee [Line 2]	$ 8,940
Priority Claims [Line 3(e)]	$ 33,762
Home Mortgage Defaults [Line 5(d)]	$ 10,800 + 864 (interest)
Long-Term Debt Defaults [Line 6(d)]	$ 372
Other Secured Claims [Line 7(d)]	$ 0
Separate Class [Line 8(b)]	$ 5,329
Unsecured Creditors[Line 9(c)]	$ 29,336
TOTAL [must equal Line 1(d)]	$ 89,403

Signed: _Martin Herchoo_
    DEBTOR

Signed: _Ellen Herchoo_
    DEBTOR (if joint case)

These forms were taken from *How to File for Chapter 7 Bankruptcy*, by Stephen Elias, Albin Renauer and Robin Leonard, and *Chapter 13 Bankruptcy: Repay Your Debts*, by Robin Leonard, both published by Nolo. Both guides contain blank forms (in addition to the filled-in samples) and complete instructions for filing a bankruptcy case on your own.

B.　Bankruptcy Petition Preparers

You may decide that you want help preparing your bankruptcy forms. In that case, you don't necessarily have to hire a lawyer. For this level of assistance, a bankruptcy petition preparer (BPP) can help you. BPPs are not lawyers, but they are familiar with the bankruptcy courts in your area. They can:

- type your forms
- help you over any rough spots you encounter when filling in the forms
- provide some basic information about local procedures and requirements, and
- help you prepare for negotiations with your creditors.

Generally, BPPs will type your bankruptcy papers for $150 or less.

BPPs are very different from lawyers. They can't give legal advice or represent you in court—only lawyers are allowed to do those things. When you use a BPP, you remain responsible for the decision-making in your case, based on the information you acquire on your own, from a lawyer or perhaps from a Nolo book such as *How to File for Chapter 7 Bankruptcy*. You cannot, legally, pass this responsibility on to a BPP.

BPPs are springing up all over the country to help people who don't want or can't afford to hire a lawyer, but you're still more likely to find a

BPP if you live on the West Coast. A recommendation from someone who has used a particular BPP is the best way to find a reputable one in your area.

BPPs often advertise in classified sections of local newspapers and in the Yellow Pages. You may have to look hard to find BPPs, however, because the Bankruptcy Code bars them from using the term "legal" or any similar term in their advertisements or from advertising under any category that contains the word "legal" or a similar term.

WHAT LAWYERS SAY ABOUT BANKRUPTCY PETITION PREPARERS

In many parts of the country, bankruptcy attorneys are extremely unhappy with the competition from BPPs. Often, the attorneys charge that BPPs are practicing law without a license or that they're incompetent. Some BPPs probably are incompetent, just as some lawyers are. But the paperwork you'll get from a BPP is probably prepared just as competently as what you'd get from a bankruptcy lawyer's office; most routine bankruptcy work in a lawyer's office is done by nonlawyer personnel anyway. How to fill out bankruptcy forms isn't taught in law school and doesn't involve any skill that lawyers (as opposed to others) necessarily possess.

C. Bankruptcy Lawyers

You may decide that you need a lawyer to help you complete the forms. Even if you think you can complete the forms on your own or by hiring a BPP, there still may be situations in which you may need a lawyer's help.

Chapter 7 bankruptcy. You may need a lawyer in a Chapter 7 bankruptcy to prepare custom-made court papers (beyond the forms shown above), to argue your side of a dispute during your bankruptcy or to negotiate with a creditor.

You may be able to hire an attorney to handle only a specific procedure while handling the main part of the bankruptcy yourself. As a general rule, you should bring an attorney into the case whenever a dispute involves something of sufficient value to justify the attorney's fees. If a creditor objects to the discharge of a $500 debt, and it will cost you $400 to hire an attorney, you may be better off trying to handle the matter yourself, even though this increases the risk that the creditor will win. If, however, the dispute is worth $1,000 and the attorney will cost you $200, hiring the attorney makes sense.

Chapter 13 bankruptcy. Becoming knowledgeable about Chapter 13 bankruptcy will require a lot of work. Chapter 13 bankruptcy is fairly complex and has no short cuts. The majority of people who file for Chapter 13 bankruptcy use an attorney, for several reasons:

- The lawyer's fee (several hundreds or thousands of dollars) can be paid through the Chapter 13 plan.
- Chapter 13 bankruptcy often requires a lot of negotiating with creditors and with the bankruptcy trustee, often to reach agreement on an acceptable repayment plan.
- Chapter 13 bankruptcy requires several court hearings or appearances.
- Chapter 13 cases have many variables. An experienced lawyer can help you understand the specifics of your case, including the types of debts you have and the amount or percentage you must repay on each.

1. How to Find a Bankruptcy Lawyer

Where there's a bankruptcy court, there are bankruptcy lawyers. They're listed in the Yellow Pages under attorneys and often advertise in newspapers. You should use an experienced bankruptcy lawyer, not a general practitioner, to advise you or handle matters associated with bankruptcy.

There are several ways to find the best bankruptcy lawyer for your job:

- **Personal referrals.** This is your best approach. If you know someone who was pleased with the services of a lawyer, call that lawyer first.
- **Bankruptcy petition preparers.** If there's a BPP in your area, chances are she works closely with bankruptcy attorneys who are both competent and sympathetic to self-helpers.

- **Legal aid.** Legal Aid offices are partially funded by the federal Legal Services Corporation and offer legal assistance in many areas; many offices do bankruptcies. To qualify for Legal Aid, you must be low income.

- **Legal clinic.** Many law schools sponsor legal clinics and provide free legal advice to consumers. Some legal clinics have the same income requirements as Legal Aid; others offer free services to low- to moderate-income people.

- **Chain law firms.** Firms such as Hyatt Legal Services routinely offer bankruptcy services.

- **Group legal plans.** If you're a member of a plan that provides legal assistance for free or low cost and the plan covers bankruptcies, check with it first for a lawyer.

- **Lawyer referral panels.** Most county bar associations will give you the names of bankruptcy attorneys who practice in your area. But bar associations usually provide only minimal screening. Take the time to check out the credentials and experience of the person to whom you're referred.

2. What to Look for in a Lawyer

No matter how you find a lawyer, here are three suggestions on how to make sure you have the best possible working relationship.

First, fight the urge you may have to surrender your will and be intimidated by a lawyer. You should be the one who decides what you feel comfortable doing about your legal and financial affairs. Keep in mind that you're hiring the lawyer to perform a service for you; shop around if the price or personality isn't right.

Second, it's important that you be as comfortable as possible with any lawyer you hire. When making an appointment, ask to talk directly to the lawyer. If you can't, this may give you a hint as to how accessible he or she is. Of course, if you're told that a paralegal will be handling the routine aspects of your case under the supervision of a lawyer, you may be satisfied with that arrangement.

If you do talk directly, ask some specific questions. Do you get clear, concise answers? If not, try someone else. Also pay attention to how the lawyer responds to your knowledge. If you've read this book, you're already better informed than most clients. Many lawyers are threatened when the client knows too much.

Finally, once you find a lawyer you like, make an hour-long appointment to discuss your situation fully. Your goal at the initial conference is to find out what the lawyer recommends and how much it will cost. Go home and think about the lawyer's suggestions. If they don't make complete sense or you have other reservations, call someone else.

3. What Bankruptcy Attorneys Charge

Fees charged by bankruptcy attorneys for a routine Chapter 7 bankruptcy vary from about $350 to $1,000 (plus the $175 filing and administrative fees). In most situations, you will have to pay the attorney in full before the attorney will file your case. Bankruptcy attorneys generally charge about $750 to $2,000 (plus the $160 filing and administrative fees) to handle an entire Chapter 13 bankruptcy case. The lawyer's fee is usually paid through the Chapter 13 plan.

You must include on your bankruptcy papers the amount you were charged by your bankruptcy lawyer. This is because every penny you pay a bankruptcy lawyer is a penny not available to your creditors. The court has the legal authority to make the attorney justify the fee. This rarely happens, however, because attorneys know the range of fees generally allowed by local bankruptcy judges and set their fees accordingly.

This means that if you were shopping around for a bankruptcy lawyer and called five lawyers in your area and asked their fees, you would be quoted very similar amounts. If the first lawyer says he would charge you $800, chances are good that the second one would charge you somewhere between $700 and $900. The third, fourth and fifth lawyers probably wouldn't differ all that much.

 Now is the time to complete the Chapter 8 questions on the "Should I File For Bankruptcy?" checklist.

Will I Be Able to Get Credit in the Future?

F or many people, the one barrier that stands between them and filing for bankruptcy is the fear that they will never get credit again. It's no wonder people feel this way. The message that creditors, particularly credit card issuers, send is that bankruptcy is the "ten year mistake."

There's no question that bankruptcy could possibly haunt you up to ten years. A bankruptcy filing can legally remain on your credit record for ten years from the date you filed your papers, although most credit bureaus remove a Chapter 13 bankruptcy filing after seven years. Major creditors, such as banks and department stores, pressured credit bureaus into removing the notations after seven years as an incentive to debtors to choose Chapter 13 bankruptcy over Chapter 7 bankruptcy.

But your bankruptcy filing will be a negative, for seven or ten years, only if you let it be. Although creditors, particularly credit card issuers, will never admit this, they readily make offers of credit to people who have been through bankruptcy. Look at it this way. After your case is over, you have no (or very little) debt and you can't file for Chapter 7 again for at least six years. You're the perfect candidate for a new credit card or loan. If you don't find the offers of credit in your mail box, go out and find them.

A. Rebuilding Your Credit

Rebuilding your credit is the process of getting positive information into your credit file so that soon after your bankruptcy, your creditors put most weight on the recent positive data and little weight on the bankruptcy and what came before it. Here are some basic steps you can take to rebuild your credit.

1. Keep Your Credit File, Accurate

When you apply for credit, the creditor will contact a credit reporting agency (also called credit bureau) and request a copy of your credit file. The information in the file is primarily what a creditor uses to decide whether to grant or deny your credit request.

So that creditors and other users of credit files see you in the best light, you want to get any incorrect or outdated information out of your credit file. Negative information that is older than seven years shouldn't be in your file, except for the bankruptcy filing, which can stay up to ten years.

For more information on rebuilding your credit—including obtaining a copy of your credit file, requesting that the credit bureau correct mistakes, contacting creditors directly for help in cleaning up your credit and getting positive information into your credit file—see *Credit Repair*, by Robin Leonard (Nolo).

2. Get Positive Information Into Your Credit File

Once your credit report is accurate (even if negative), you want to get some positive information into your credit file. One way is to use a credit card.

If you've hung onto a bank, department store or gasoline credit card through your bankruptcy case, use that card. Otherwise, you can take advantage to the offers you get after your bankruptcy case is over, or you can apply at a local bank. If you don't qualify for a regular card, look for something called a secured card. This requires that you deposit money into a savings account in exchange for the credit card. You have no access to the savings account. If you don't pay your bill, the bank uses the money in your account to cover what you owe.

Credit cards aren't the only source of positive data for a credit file. Consider a bank loan. A few banks offer something called a passbook savings loan, which is a lot like a secured credit card. You deposit a sum of money into a savings account, and in exchange the bank makes you a loan. You have no access to your savings account while your loan is outstanding. If you don't repay it, the bank will use the money in your savings account.

In most cases, though, you'll have to apply for a standard bank loan. You may need a cosigner or to offer some property as collateral.

CREDIT REPAIR AGENCIES

You've probably seen ads for companies that claim they can fix your credit, qualify you for a loan and get you a credit card. Stay clear of these companies—many of their practices are illegal. Some steal the credit files or Social Security numbers of people who have died or live in places like Guam or the U.S. Virgin Islands and replace your file with these other files. Others create new identities for debtors by applying to the IRS for a taxpayer I.D. number and telling debtors to use it in place of their Social Security number.

But even the legitimate companies can't do anything for you that you can't do yourself. If items in your credit file are correct, these companies cannot get them removed. If items are incorrect, they follow the same steps outlined above. About the only difference between using a legitimate credit repair agency and doing it yourself is saving a few thousands of dollars those agencies charge.

Once you've started rebuilding your credit, you will find that creditors generally ignore your bankruptcy after two or three years. Over time, it will become increasingly easy to qualify for a personal loan, car loan and even mortgage. Mortgages, especially, aren't that difficult to get, even if you've been through bankruptcy. You may pay slightly higher interest or more points, or may be required to put 20% or more down, but you should get a loan, assuming you can afford the monthly payments. Lenders like making home loans, which are quite secure.

B. Where You May Run Into Problems

People who work in the financial industry tend to understand what bankruptcy is and why people file. While they may not want you to go bankrupt on their debts, they are often forgiving of people who have faced financial hardship and decided to take care of it through bankruptcy. They also know that you can't file again for a while and that therefore there's a very high probability that you will pay back any new loan or extension of credit.

Unfortunately, people who don't work in the financial industry are fairly clueless about what bankruptcy is and why people file. They often make the assumption that only deadbeats and poor money managers go bankrupt. If you encounter one of these people, your life can be miserable. You may be denied a job or a rental place to live if the person doing the hiring or renting gets wind of your bankruptcy.

In fact, the most common problem encountered by people who have been through bankruptcy is in renting a place to live. If a potential landlord does a credit check, sees your bankruptcy and refuses to rent to you, there's not much you can do other than try to show that you'll pay your rent and be a responsible tenant. You probably will need to go apartment hunting with a "renter's resume" that shows you in the best possible light. Be ready to offer a cosigner, to find roommates or to pay several months rent up front in cash.

Now is the time to complete the Chapter 9 questions on the "Should I File For Bankruptcy?" checklist.

Can Some Alternative Outside of Bankruptcy Do the Trick?

I f you've read the previous nine chapters, you may be leaning toward filing for bankruptcy. Before you conclude with certainty that bankruptcy is the right solution, take the time to read this chapter. While for some people filing for bankruptcy is the only sensible remedy for debt problems, for many others another course of action makes better sense.

A. Do Nothing

Surprisingly, the best approach for some people deeply in debt is to take no action at all. You can't be thrown in jail for not paying your debts, except in the unusual situations described in Chapter 7.

Furthermore, unless a creditor sues you and obtains a judgment, the creditor can't come to your house and start grabbing items. The one exception is if you default on a secured debt—and then the creditor can take only the property that secures the debt. Nor can any creditor except the IRS empty your bank account without first suing you and obtaining a judgment.

Even if creditors get a judgment, they can't take away such essentials as basic clothing, ordinary household furnishings, personal effects, food, Social Security, unemployment benefits, public assistance or 75% of your wages. The state exemptions described in Chapters 4 and 5 apply both if you file for bankruptcy or a creditor sues you and gets a judgment against you. (Neither the federal bankruptcy exemptions nor the California System 2 exemptions apply if a creditor sues you. Those are bankruptcy-only exemptions.) If all of the property you own is exempt, you are known as "judgment-proof." Whoever sues you and wins will be holding a useless piece of paper, simply because you don't have anything that can legally be taken.

If your creditors know that it's unlikely they could collect a judgment, they probably won't sue you. Instead, they'll simply write off your debt and treat it as a deductible business loss for income tax purposes. In several years (usually between six and ten), the debt will become legally uncollectible under a state law called the statute of limitations.

STOPPING BILL COLLECTOR ABUSE AND HARASSMENT

You don't need to file for bankruptcy just to get annoying collection agencies off your back. Federal law forbids them from threatening you, lying about what they can do to you or invading your privacy. Under this law, you can also legally force collection agencies to stop phoning or writing you simply by demanding that they stop, even if you owe them a bundle and can't pay a cent. (The law is the federal Fair Debt Collections Practices Act, 15 U.S §1692 and following.) For more information, see *Money Troubles: Legal Strategies to Cope With Your Debts,* by Robin Leonard (Nolo).

B. Negotiate With Your Creditors

If you have some income, or you have assets you're willing to sell, you may be a lot better off negotiating with your creditors than filing for bankruptcy. Negotiation may simply buy you some time to get back on your feet, or you and your creditors may agree on a complete settlement of your debts for less than you owe.

Creditors hate it when debtors don't pay their debts. This forces creditors to institute collection proceedings, a process that turns the debtor into a former customer. To avoid the collection process and to keep customers, creditors often will reduce payments, extend time to pay, drop late fees and make similar adjustments if they believe you are making an honest effort to deal with your debt problems.

As soon as it becomes clear to you that you're going to have trouble paying a bill, write to the creditor. Explain the problem—accident, job layoff, emergency expense for your child, unexpected tax bill or whatever. Mention any development that points to an encouraging financial condition, such as job prospects. Also, consider sending a token payment. This tells the creditor that you are serious about paying but just can't now.

Your success with getting creditors to give you time to pay will depend on the types of debts you have, how far behind you are and the creditors' policies toward debts that are in arrears.

If you are not yet behind on your bills, be aware that a number of creditors have a ridiculous policy that requires you to default—and in some cases, become at least 90 days past due—before they will negotiate with you. If any creditor makes this a condition of negotiating, find out from the creditor how you can keep the default out of your credit report.

In addition, increasing numbers of creditors simply will not negotiate with debtors. Despite the fact that creditors get at least something when they negotiate settlements with debtors, many ignore debtors' pleas for help, continue to call demanding payment and leave debtors with few options other than filing for bankruptcy. In fact, nearly one-third of the people who filed for bankruptcy during the mid-1990s stated that the final straw that sent them into bankruptcy was the unreasonableness of their creditors or the collection agencies hired by their creditors.

Despite this trend, it is still in your best interest to contact your creditors and try to negotiate. Not all creditors are unreasonable. Furthermore, as this trend becomes more widely known, some creditors may change their ways to avoid embarrassment—and possibly to avoid the wrath of their shareholders who may be angry that the creditor opted to receive nothing rather than something.

How to negotiate with creditors and collection agencies, and how to stop bill collector abuse, is covered in detail in *Money Troubles: Legal Strategies to Cope With Your Debts*, by Robin Leonard (Nolo). That book covers how to deal with creditors when you owe money on credit cards, mortgage loans, car loans, child support and alimony, among other debts.

C. Get Outside Help to Design a Repayment Plan

Credit and debt counseling agencies are nonprofit organizations funded primarily by major creditors, such as department stores, credit card companies and banks, who can work with you to help you repay your debts and improve your financial picture.

To use a credit or debt counseling agency to help you pay your debts, you must have some disposable income. A counselor contacts your creditors to let them know that you've sought assistance and need more time to pay. Based on your income and debts, the counselor, with your creditors, decides on how much you pay. You then make one payment each month to the counseling agency, which in turn pays your creditors. The agency asks the creditors to return a small percentage of the money received to the agency office to fund its work. This arrangement is generally referred to as a debt management program.

Some creditors will make overtures to help you when you're on a debt management program. For example, Citicorp waives minimum payment and late charges—and may freeze interest assessments—for customers undergoing credit counseling. But few creditors will make interest concessions, such as waiving a portion of the accumulated interest to help you repay the principal. More likely, you'll get late fees dropped and the opportunity to reinstate your credit if you successfully complete a debt management program.

The combination of high consumer debt and easy access to information (the Internet) has led to an explosion in the number of credit and debt counseling agencies ready to offer you help. Some provide limited services, such as budgeting and debt repayment, while others offer a range of services, from debt counseling to financial planning.

Participating in a credit or debt counseling agency's debt management program is a little bit like filing for Chapter 13 bankruptcy. (See Chapter 1, Section C.5.) Working with a credit or debt counseling agency has one advantage: no bankruptcy will appear on your credit record.

But a debt management program also has two disadvantages when compared to Chapter 13 bankruptcy. First, if you miss a payment, Chapter 13 protects you from creditors who would start collection actions. A debt management program has no such protection and any one creditor can pull the plug on your plan. Also, a debt management program plan usually requires that your debts be paid in full. In Chapter 13 bankruptcy, you're required to pay the value of your nonexempt property, which can mean that you pay only a small fraction of your unsecured debts.

Critics of credit and debt counseling agencies point out that they get most of their funding from creditors. (Some offices also receive grants from private agencies such as the United Way and federal agencies including the Department of Housing and Urban Development.) Nevertheless, critics claim that counselors cannot be objective in counseling debtors to file for bankruptcy if they know the office won't receive any funds.

In response to this and other consumer concerns, credit and debt counseling agencies accredited by the National Foundation for Consumer Credit (the majority of agencies are) reached an agreement with the Federal Trade Commission to disclose the following to consumers:

- that creditors fund a large portion of the cost of their operations
- that the credit agency must balance the ability of the debtor to make payments with the requirements of the creditors that fund the office, and
- a reliable estimate of how long it will take a debtor to repay his or her debts under a debt management program.

1. Consumer Credit Counseling Service

Consumer Credit Counseling Service (CCCS) is the oldest credit or debt counseling agency in the country. Actually, CCCS isn't one agency. CCCS is the primary operating name of many credit and debt counseling agencies affiliated with the National Foundation for Consumer Credit (NFCC).

CCCS may charge you a small monthly fee (an average of about $9) for setting up a repayment plan. CCCS also helps people make monthly budgets, and sometimes charges a one-time fee of about $20. If you can't afford the fee, CCCS will waive it. In most CCCS offices, the primary service offered is a debt management program. A few offices have additional services, such as helping you save money toward buying a house or reviewing your credit report.

CCCS has more than 1,100 offices, located in every state. Look in the phone book to find the one nearest you or contact the main office at 8611 2nd Avenue, Suite 100, Silver Spring, MD 20910, 800-388-2227 (voice).

2. Debt Counselors of America

Debt Counselors of America (DCA) offers budgeting and debt management programs, like other debt and credit counseling agencies. But unlike most other agencies, DCA has a financial planning department with Certified Financial Planners and a Crisis Relief Team to assist consumers who are turned away by other credit or debt counseling agencies or who have very complex problems. DCA is also the first credit or debt counseling agency that is a registered investment advisor. Each week, DCA broadcasts a live call-in radio show over its Internet site, where you can also find numerous publications on a range of money issues.

DCA has only one office. That's because DCA offers its services via phone, fax, e-mail and the Internet. You can contact DCA at 1680 East Gude Drive, Rockville, MD 20850, 800-680-3328 (voice), 301-762-6344 (fax), counselor@mail.dca.org (e-mail) or http://www.dca.org (Internet).

3. Other Credit and Debt Counseling Agencies

Surf the Internet and you'll find many other credit and debt counseling agencies offering a variety of services. Be sure to ask questions about their services before signing up.

Three agencies with national recognition are as follows:

Genus Credit Management

10500 Little Patuxent Parkway
Columbia, MD 21044
888-793-4368 (voice)
410-997-5368 (fax)
http://www.genus.org (Internet)

Genus offers a debt management program, with payments deducted automatically from your checking or savings account. Genus also provides mortgage repayment assistance, publications, videos, a monthly newsletter and workshops.

Money Management International
4600 Gulf Freeway, Suite 500
Houston, TX 77023
800-762-2271 (voice)
http://www.moneymanagementbymail.org (Internet)

MMI provides credit counseling, debt management, and economic education information by telephone, e-mail, fax and mail, 24 hours a day, seven days a week. MMI's Internet site includes a debt counseling application and message board where you can send your money questions to "Letters to Susan and Co."

The Center for Debt Management
Family Debt Arbitration and Counseling Services, Inc.
P.O. Box 99
Candia, NH 03034
603-483-0593 (voice)
603-483-0572 (fax)
http://members.aol.com/DebtRelief/index.html (Internet)

CDM offers several services on its Internet site:

- debt counseling—answers to your questions
- debt management—repayment plan
- publications—topics include bankruptcy, debt consolidation, credit cards, credit bureaus, credit repair, collection agencies, student loans, financial aid, government programs, law and more
- words of wisdom—words of inspiration and noteworthy quotations related to getting out of debt, and
- consumer information—consumer alerts and links to consumer protection agencies and other sites of interest.

D. File for Chapter 11 Bankruptcy

Chapter 11 bankruptcy is the type of bankruptcy used by financially struggling businesses to reorganize their affairs. It is also available to individuals. Individuals who consider Chapter 11 bankruptcy usually have debts in excess of one or both of the Chapter 13 bankruptcy limits—$269,250 of unsecured debts and $807,750 of secured debts—or substantial nonexempt assets, such as several pieces of real estate.

The initial filing fee is currently $830, compared to $200 for Chapter 7 or $185 for Chapter 13 bankruptcy. In addition, you must pay a quarterly fee that is a percentage of your debts (often several hundreds or thousands of dollars) until your reorganization plan is approved or dismissed, or your case is converted to Chapter 7 bankruptcy. Most attorneys require a minimum $7,500 retainer fee to handle a Chapter 11 bankruptcy case. Add to that the Chapter 11 bankruptcy court fees, which one year after you file could run you $10,000. If you want to read more on this kind of bankruptcy, see *A Feast for Lawyers*, by Sol Stein (Evans, M., & Co. Inc.).

 You'll need a lawyer to file for Chapter 11 bankruptcy. A Chapter 11 bankruptcy often turns into a long, expensive, lawyer-infested mess, and many Chapter 11 filings end up being converted to Chapter 7 bankruptcy. Even to file a "fast-track" Chapter 11 bankruptcy for small businesses with debts up to $2 million, you will need an attorney.

E. File for Chapter 12 Bankruptcy

Chapter 12 bankruptcy is almost identical to Chapter 13 bankruptcy. To be eligible for Chapter 12 bankruptcy, however, at least 80% of your debts must arise from the operation of a family farm. The fee for filing a Chapter 12 case is $230.

 See a lawyer if you want to file for Chapter 12 bankruptcy.

Now is the time to complete the Chapter 10 questions on the "Should I File For Bankruptcy?" checklist.

What If the Bankruptcy Law Changes?

Almost annually, Congress considers legislation that would significantly change the consumer bankruptcy laws—both Chapter 7 and Chapter 13. The intent of those who support bankruptcy reform is to make it harder to file for Chapter 7 bankruptcy and increase payments to creditors in both Chapter 7 bankruptcy and Chapter 13 bankruptcy.

This chapter summarizes just a few of the provisions contained in the bills debated in the late 1990s and in early 2000. Keep in mind that any new bill may be very different. You can download copies of bills at http://thomas.loc.gov. Analyses of the bills and day-by-day news updates are available on the Website maintained by the American Bankruptcy Institute at http://www.abiworld.org.

A. Needs-Based Chapter 7 Bankruptcy

There is no question that a major impetus behind bankruptcy reform is the substantial increase in consumer bankruptcy filings—they have exceeded one million since 1996. Any reform bill out of Congress will make it more difficult to file a Chapter 7 case.

The House and Senate have both shown support for what is referred to as "needs-based" bankruptcy. The idea behind needs-based bankruptcy is that if your annual income is at or below the federal poverty level ($9,260 for one person and $12,480 for a family of two in 1998), you would automatically qualify to file a Chapter 7 bankruptcy. If your income is more than the federal poverty level, you will be allowed to file for Chapter 7 bankruptcy only if you meet a means test. One House bill spelled out a test formula:

1. Figure out your average monthly income from all sources for the past six months.

2. Subtract from the amount in Step 1 the following:

   a. The total of all payments on secured debts, such as mortgages and car loans, that you'd be required to make over the next five years divided by 60. (Secured debts are explained in Chapter 2, Section B.4.a.)

   b. The total of all payments on priority debts, such as child support and most income taxes, that you'd be required to make over the next five years divided by 60. (Priority debts are defined in Chapter 1, Section A.2.)

   c. Monthly living expenses for you and your dependents according to standards established by the IRS for purposes of collecting unpaid taxes. These expenses fall into three basic categories— housing and utilities; transportation; and food, clothing and other items. The amounts are hardly generous and, for most people, do not reflect the actual cost of living.

3. If the amount you get by subtracting your expenses (Step 2) from your income (Step 1) is $50 or less, you will be allowed to file a Chapter 7 bankruptcy. If the amount is more than $50, you must multiply it by 60 to determine the amount you could pay your creditors for five years. If this amount is at least 20% of your unsecured debts, you would be barred from filing for Chapter 7 bankruptcy. (Unsecured debts are defined in Chapter 2, Section B.4.b.) You would have to file a Chapter 13 case or deal with your debts outside of bankruptcy.

Senate bills have also contained a need-based bankruptcy provision, but do not include a means test. Instead, they simply give the bankruptcy judge the authority to dismiss a Chapter 7 case or convert it to a Chapter 13 bankruptcy if granting relief under Chapter 7 of the Bankruptcy Code would be an abuse of the bankruptcy system. Although abuse is undefined, the judge must consider two factors:

- your ability, based on your current income, to pay 20% of more of your unsecured debt, and

- whether you filed your bankruptcy case in bad faith (also undefined).

Suffice it to say that if a bankruptcy reform bill emerges from Congress, it will probably contain a provision barring anyone who has the ability to repay at least 20% of his or her unsecured debts (according to a formula or a bankruptcy judge) from filing a Chapter 7 bankruptcy.

B.   Longer Chapter 13 Bankruptcies

Currently, most Chapter 13 bankruptcy repayment plans last three years. If necessary, a judge can extend this to as many as five years. Under some bills, most plans would have lasted five years and, with court approval, as many as seven years. Low-income debtors would be able to propose three-year repayment plans.

C.   Participation in Credit Counseling

Under most bills, you would have to present the bankruptcy court with a certificate from a nonprofit credit counseling agency registered with the bankruptcy court stating that you made a good faith attempt to repay your debts through a credit counseling service before filing for bankruptcy. The only exceptions would be if there was no suitable credit counseling service available in your area or if a creditor or debt collector was about to grab your property.

D. New Nondischargeable Debts

Under current law, if, within the 60 days before filing for bankruptcy, you incur debts of more than $1,075 to one creditor for luxury goods or services or take cash advances totaling more than $1,075, the debts are presumed to have been incurred fraudulently and are nondischargeable if a creditor objects. Most bills would change this presumption to all consumer debts incurred within 90 days before filing for bankruptcy. Some bills include an exception for small amounts of debts for necessities—such as under $500.

Under another provision contained in most bills, certain debts would no longer have been dischargeable in Chapter 13 bankruptcy. As explained in Chapter 3, if at the end of a Chapter 13 repayment plan you still owe a balance on debts from fraud, debts from willful and malicious acts or debts from embezzlement, larceny or breach of fiduciary duty, the balance is wiped out under Chapter 13 bankruptcy's "superdischarge." The superdischarge applied to these debts may be eliminated.

Under current law, any *nonsupport* debt arising from a separation agreement or divorce, or in connection with a marital settlement agreement, divorce decree or other court order, can be considered nondischargeable in a Chapter 7 case. (See Chapter 3, Section A.2.d.) Furthermore, any balance on these debts remaining at the end of a Chapter 13 case is wiped out by the superdischarge. Under some bills considered by Congress, these debts would be completely nondischargeable under all circumstances.

E. Extended Time Between Filings

Currently, you are barred from filing for Chapter 7 bankruptcy if you received a Chapter 7 discharge within the previous six years. There is no similar limit for filing a Chapter 13 case. Under some bills considered by Congress, you would not be able to file a Chapter 7 case if you received a Chapter 7 discharge within the previous ten years, and you would have been barred from filing a Chapter 13 bankruptcy if you received either a Chapter 7 or Chapter 13 discharge within the previous five years.

F. Random Audits

Most bills establish a system for random audits by independent public accountants of 1%-2% of all cases filed to determine the accuracy and completeness of the forms filed and other information you provide in a bankruptcy. None of the bills indicated the source of funding. Most likely, it would be through the fees collected from debtors at the time of filing and from any creditors seeking relief from the automatic stay. (The automatic stay is explained in Chapter 1, Sections B, D.1.b and D.2.d.) Given how few creditors file a motion to have the stay lifted, the most likely outcome would be an increase in filing fees.

G. Attachment of Tax Returns and Other Information

Chapter 8, Section A provides the list of forms that must be filed in every Chapter 7 bankruptcy or Chapter 13 bankruptcy. Under most bills considered by Congress, those forms would not be enough. You'd be required to include copies of all federal tax returns filed during the three years before you file for bankruptcy and your pay stubs or other evidence of payment from your employer for the two months prior to filing. If you haven't filed tax returns for the years in question, you would have to do so in order to be eligible to file a Chapter 13 bankruptcy. In addition, during a Chapter 13 case, you would be required to provide annual updates of your income and expenses.

H. Homestead Exemption Limit

Some bills seek to cap the homestead exemption (except for family farmers) at $100,000. (The homestead exemption is discussed in Chapter 4, Section A.1.b.) While this would increase the exemption in many states, the intent is to reduce it in states that have unlimited homestead exemptions, such as Arkansas, Florida, Iowa, Kansas, Oklahoma, South Dakota and Texas.

 Now is the time to complete the Chapter 11 questions on the "Should I File For Bankruptcy?" checklist.

CHECKLIST: SHOULD I FILE FOR BANKRUPTCY?

Chapter 1: What Is Bankruptcy?	Yes, describes my situation	No, that's not my situation
My debts are too much for me to handle.	✓	
My creditors are ruining my life.	✓	

Comment: If your debts are too much for you to handle, this may be justification enough for you to file for bankruptcy. Before you do, however, make sure that bankruptcy will get rid of or help you get a handle on your debts (Chapter 3) and that there isn't another option you could use to achieve the same result (Chapter 10).

If your creditors are making your life miserable, bankruptcy will stop them cold. Certain types of creditors can get permission from the bankruptcy court to resume collection efforts after you file, however. So before you file, make sure that bankruptcy will keep the creditors you're worried about off your back (Chapter 1, Section B).

Chapter 2: Who Can File for Bankruptcy?	Yes, describes my situation	No, that's not my situation
I qualify for Chapter 7 bankruptcy—I did not receive a bankruptcy discharge during the previous six years nor was a bankruptcy case dismissed against me during the previous 180 days.	✓	
I qualify for Chapter 13 bankruptcy—I have regular and disposable income and my debts aren't too high.		✓

Comment: If both of these statements describe your situation, then you qualify for both types of bankruptcy and need to figure out which one makes more sense given your situation (Chapter 1, Section A, can help). If only one statement describes your situation, then you are limited to filing that one type of bankruptcy—but again, only if it makes sense to do so.

Chapter 3: Will I Wipe Out My Debts?	Yes, describes my situation	No, that's not my situation
I could eliminate or substantially reduce my debts.	✓	
There's little chance creditors would object to my bankruptcy.	✓	
I'm not concerned about sticking a codebtor with a debt.	✓	

Comment: Chapter 7 bankruptcy is a powerful remedy to get rid of your debts. But if you use it now, you will be barred from filing another Chapter 7 case for six years. Make sure you've stopped incurring debt and that you'll be able to wipe out or substantially reduce your debts by filing. Also, if you have good reason to believe that a creditor will object to your case, or that you'll be sticking it to a codebtor, Chapter 7 bankruptcy may be a less attractive option—you'll probably want to weigh all of the pros and cons presented on this checklist.

Chapter 4: Will I Lose My House or Apartment?	Yes, describes my situation	No, that's not my situation
I have little or nonexempt equity in my house (Chapter 7 consideration only).	✓	
I'm current on my mortgage or rent payments, or I could get current either before I file or during my case.	✓	

Comment: Under bankruptcy's technical rules, your choice to file or not to file, or to file a Chapter 7 case versus a Chapter 13 case, could determine whether or not you get to keep your house. If holding on to your house is important to you, make sure you understand the concepts of "equity," "homestead exemption" and "foreclosure" before proceeding. Similarly, if you are considering filing for bankruptcy to avoid an eviction, be sure you understand the limits of this strategy.

Chapter 5: Can I Keep My Car and Other Vital Items of Property?	Yes, describes my situation	No, that's not my situation
I'm not likely to lose my car.	✓	
I'm not likely to lose the tools of my trade.	✓	
I'm not likely to lose my pension.	✓	
I have no or very little other property I'm likely to lose.	✓	
I might lose some property, but I can live with that.		✓

Comment: In general, very few debtors give up any property in a Chapter 7 bankruptcy. Similarly, Chapter 13 bankruptcy is designed so that you don't lose any property and instead use income to repay your debts. But these are general rules. If you have property you desperately want to hold on to, make sure you understand the exemption rules for your state; how Chapter 7 bankruptcy deals with secured property, such as a car subject to a car note; and how you can use Chapter 13 bankruptcy to make up the arrears owed on a secured debt.

Chapter 6: Can I Keep My Credit Cards?	Yes, describes my situation	No, that's not my situation
I'm not current on my credit cards, so trying to keep them through bankruptcy isn't a concern for me.		✓
I'm current on a credit card, but I don't care if I lose it.	✓	
I don't think my credit card issuers could successfully object to my discharging their debts—I haven't incurred credit card debt recently, I wasn't insolvent when I incurred credit card debt and I always intended to repay my credit card debts.	✓	

Comment: The desire to hold on to a credit card should not be a deciding factor in determining whether or not to file for bankruptcy. If you're concerned that a creditor might object to your bankruptcy case or at least to the discharge of a credit card debt, however, you may want to explore the likelihood of this—or more importantly, the likelihood of the creditor succeeding—before you file.

Chapter 7: Will I Lose My Job, Children, Freedom or Self-Respect?	Yes, describes my situation	No, that's not my situation
I'm not worried that bankruptcy will affect my ability to get a job in the future.		✓
I'm not contemplating a divorce (Chapter 13 consideration only).	✓	
I'm not concerned about neighbors or others in my community finding out.	✓	

Comment: Saving face can be a powerful motivator in our culture. Only you can decide if these potential harms—such as people in your community possibly learning of your bankruptcy—outweigh the benefits.

Chapter 8: Is It Too Hard to File?	Yes, describes my situation	No, that's not my situation
I think I can file on my own.		✓
I can afford to pay a lawyer or BPP the full amount when I file.	✓	
I want to pay the lawyer's fee over time (Chapter 13 consideration only).		✓

Comment: Filing a Chapter 7 bankruptcy on one's own usually is not difficult. But if filing on your own seems overwhelming or simply isn't what you want to do, you may be able to find an inexpensive alternative to using a lawyer—a bankruptcy petition preparer. If using a lawyer seems absolutely necessary and you can't afford to pay the lawyer's fee all at once, Chapter 13 bankruptcy gives you the option to pay it off over time with your other debts.

Chapter 9: Will I Be Able to Get Credit in the Future?	Yes, describes my situation	No, that's not my situation
I don't care about getting credit any time soon.		✓
I'm confident I will be able to improve my credit after my case is over.	✓	
I'm not likely to need to find new rental housing anytime soon.		✓

Comment: Many creditors will tell you that you won't be able to get credit in the future if you file for bankruptcy. There is almost no truth to this statement.

Chapter 10: Can Some Alternative Outside of Bankruptcy Do the Trick?	Yes, describes my situation	No, that's not my situation
I'm not judgment proof.		✓
My creditors won't negotiate with me.	✓	
A debt counseling agency can't or won't help me.	✓	

Comment: Bankruptcy is a powerful remedy. Make sure it's the one you really need.

Chapter 11: What If the Bankruptcy Law Changes?	Yes, describes my situation	No, that's not my situation
I would no longer qualify under a "needs-based bankruptcy."	✓	✓
I can't imagine being in Chapter 13 bankruptcy for as long as seven years.	✓	
I have debts I incurred within the past 90 days I need to discharge.	✓	
I received a Chapter 7 discharge within the previous ten years.		✓

Comment: If the law changed and you would no longer qualify for bankruptcy or you might not benefit as much as you could under the current law, you will want to file as soon as possible—if you've concluded that bankruptcy is the right solution for you.

Final Considerations	Yes, describes my situation	No, that's not my situation
The benefits of bankruptcy outweigh what I might give up.	✓	
I still have questions about bankruptcy that this book doesn't answer.	✓	

Comment: Deciding whether or not to file for bankruptcy almost always involves weighing the pros and cons. If your debts are unmanageable, and you'll be likely to get rid of your debts while keeping your property, then the more it may make sense to file. If, however, you think you could pay off your debts outside of bankruptcy if you worked hard at it, or if you won't eliminate enough debts or you might lose property you really want to keep, then it may make little sense to file.

If you have questions or concerns that this book doesn't answer, you owe it to yourself to get answers before filing for bankruptcy. Bankruptcy lawyers are one good source of information. So are Nolo's other bankruptcy publications, *How to File for Chapter 7 Bankruptcy* or *Chapter 13 Bankruptcy: Repay Your Debts*. If you're willing to do some research in a law library or on the Internet, you may find the answers for yourself. The bottom line? Don't file for bankruptcy, or choose a particular form of bankruptcy, unless you're convinced it's the right thing to do.

Index

CATALOG

		PRICE	CODE

BUSINESS

	PRICE	CODE
Avoid Employee Lawsuits (Quick & Legal Series)	$24.95	AVEL
⊙ The CA Nonprofit Corp Kit (Binder w/CD-ROM)	$49.95	CNP
▣ Consultant & Independent Contractor Agreements (Book w/Disk—PC)	$24.95	CICA
▣ The Corporate Minutes Book (Book w/Disk—PC)	$69.95	CORMI
The Employer's Legal Handbook	$39.95	EMPL
▣ Form Your Own Limited Liability Company (Book w/Disk—PC)	$44.95	LIAB
▣ Hiring Independent Contractors: The Employer's Legal Guide (Book w/Disk—PC)	$34.95	HICI
▣ How to Create a Buy-Sell Agreement & Control the Destiny of your Small Business (Book w/Disk—PC)	$49.95	BSAG
▣ How to Form a California Professional Corporation (Book w/Disk—PC)	$49.95	PROF
▣ How to Form a Nonprofit Corporation (Book w/Disk—PC)—National Edition (CA edition also available)	$44.95	NNP
▣ How to Form Your Own California Corporation (Book w/Disk—PC) (NY & TX editions also available)	$39.95	CCOR
How to Write a Business Plan	$29.95	SBS
The Independent Paralegal's Handbook	$29.95	PARA
Legal Guide for Starting & Running a Small Business, Vol. 1	$29.95	RUNS
▣ Legal Guide for Starting & Running a Small Business, Vol. 2: Legal Forms (Book w/Disk—PC)	$29.95	RUNS2
Marketing Without Advertising	$22.00	MWAD
▣ Music Law (Book w/Disk—PC)	$29.95	ML
Nolo's California Quick Corp (Quick & Legal Series)	$19.95	QINC
⊙ Open Your California Business in 24 Hours (Book w/CD-ROM)	$24.95	OPEN
▣ The Partnership Book: How to Write a Partnership Agreement (Book w/Disk—PC)	$39.95	PART
Sexual Harassment on the Job	$24.95	HARS
Starting & Running a Successful Newsletter or Magazine	$29.95	MAG
Take Charge of Your California Workers' Compensation Claim	$34.95	WORK
Tax Savvy for Small Business	$34.95	SAVVY
Wage Slave No More: Law & Taxes for the Self-Employed	$24.95	WAGE
▣ Your Limited Liability Company: An Operating Manual (Book w/Disk—PC)	$49.95	LOP
Your Rights in the Workplace	$24.95	YRW

CONSUMER

	PRICE	CODE
How to Win Your Personal Injury Claim	$29.95	PICL
Nolo's Everyday Law Book	$24.95	EVL
Nolo's Pocket Guide to California Law	$15.95	CLAW
Trouble-Free Travel...And What to Do When Things Go Wrong	$14.95	TRAV

ESTATE PLANNING & PROBATE

	PRICE	CODE
8 Ways to Avoid Probate (Quick & Legal Series)	$16.95	PRO8
9 Ways to Avoid Estate Taxes (Quick & Legal Series)	$24.95	ESTX
Estate Planning Basics (Quick & Legal Series)	$18.95	ESPN
How to Probate an Estate in California	$39.95	PAE
▣ Make Your Own Living Trust (Book w/Disk—PC)	$34.95	LITR
Nolo's Law Form Kit: Wills	$19.95	KWL
▣ Nolo's Will Book (Book w/Disk—PC)	$34.95	SWIL
Plan Your Estate	$34.95	NEST
Quick & Legal Will Book (Quick & Legal Series)	$21.95	QUIC

▣ Book with disk   ⊙ Book with CD-ROM

	PRICE	CODE

FAMILY MATTERS

	PRICE	CODE
Child Custody: Building Parenting Agreements That Work	$29.95	CUST
Child Support in California: Go to Court to Get More or Pay Less (Quick & Legal Series)	$24.95	CHLD
The Complete IEP Guide	$24.95	IEP
Divorce & Money: How to Make the Best Financial Decisions During Divorce	$34.95	DIMO
Get a Life: You Don't Need a Million to Retire Well	$19.95	LIFE
The Guardianship Book for California	$34.95	GB
⊙ How to Adopt Your Stepchild in California (Book w/CD-ROM)	$34.95	ADOP
A Legal Guide for Lesbian and Gay Couples	$25.95	LG
▣ Living Together (Book w/Disk—PC)	$34.95	LTK
Nolo's Pocket Guide to Family Law	$14.95	FLD
Using Divorce Mediation: Save Your Money & Your Sanity	$21.95	UDMD

GOING TO COURT

	PRICE	CODE
Beat Your Ticket: Go To Court and Win! (National Edition—California edition also available)	$19.95	BEYT
The Criminal Law Handbook: Know Your Rights, Survive the System	$29.95	KYR
Everybody's Guide to Small Claims Court (National Edition—California edition also available)	$18.95	NSCC
How to Change Your Name in California	$34.95	NAME
How to Collect When You Win a Lawsuit (California Edition)	$29.95	JUDG
How to Mediate Your Dispute	$18.95	MEDI
How to Seal Your Juvenile & Criminal Records (California Edition)	$29.95	CRIM
How to Sue for Up to $25,000...and Win! (California Edition)	$29.95	MUNI
Mad at Your Lawyer	$21.95	MAD
Nolo's Deposition Handbook	$29.95	DEP
Represent Yourself in Court: How to Prepare & Try a Winning Case	$29.95	RYC

HOMEOWNERS, LANDLORDS & TENANTS

	PRICE	CODE
California Tenants' Rights	$24.95	CTEN
▣ Contractors' and Homeowners' Guide to Mechanics' Liens (Book w/Disk—PC)	$39.95	MIEN
The Deeds Book (California Edition)	$24.95	DEED
Dog Law	$14.95	DOG
⊙ Every Landlord's Legal Guide (National Edition, Book w/CD-ROM)	$44.95	ELLI
Every Tenant's Legal Guide	$26.95	EVTEN
For Sale by Owner in California	$24.95	FSBO
How to Buy a House in California	$24.95	BHCA
The Landlord's Law Book, Vol. 1: Rights & Responsibilities (California Edition)	$44.95	LBRT
⊙ The California Landlord's Law Book, Vol. 2: Evictions (Book w/CD-ROM)	$44.95	LBEV
Leases & Rental Agreements (Quick & Legal Series)	$24.95	LEAR
Neighbor Law: Fences, Trees, Boundaries & Noise	$24.95	NEI
⊙ The New York Landlord's Law Book (Book w/CD-ROM)	$39.95	NYLL
Renters' Rights (National Edition—Quick & Legal Series)	$19.95	RENT
Stop Foreclosure Now in California	$34.95	CLOS

IMMIGRATION/LEGAL RESEARCH

	PRICE	CODE
How to Get a Green Card: Legal Ways to Stay in the U.S.A.	$29.95	GRN
U.S. Immigration Made Easy	$44.95	IMEZ
Legal Research: How to Find & Understand the Law	$29.95	LRES

MONEY MATTERS

	PRICE	CODE
▣ 101 Law Forms for Personal Use (Quick & Legal Series, Book w/disk—PC)	$29.95	SPOT
Bankruptcy: Is It the Right Solution to Your Debt Problems? (Quick & Legal Series)	$19.95	BRS
Chapter 13 Bankruptcy: Repay Your Debts	$29.95	CH13

▣ Book with disk   ⊙ Book with CD-ROM

	PRICE	CODE
⊡ Credit Repair (Quick & Legal Series, Book w/disk—PC)	$18.95	CREP
⊡ The Financial Power of Attorney Workbook (Book w/disk—PC)	$29.95	FINPOA
How to File for Chapter 7 Bankruptcy	$29.95	HFB
IRAs, 401(k)s & Other Retirement Plans: Taking Your Money Out	$24.95	RET
Money Troubles: Legal Strategies to Cope With Your Debts	$24.95	MT
Nolo's Law Form Kit: Personal Bankruptcy	$16.95	KBNK
Stand Up to the IRS	$29.95	SIRS
Surviving an IRS Tax Audit (Quick & Legal Series)	$24.95	SAUD
Take Control of Your Student Loan Debt	$24.95	SLOAN

PATENTS AND COPYRIGHTS

	PRICE	CODE
⊙ The Copyright Handbook: How to Protect and Use Written Works (Book w/CD-ROM)	$34.95	COHA
Copyright Your Software	$24.95	CYS
⊡ Getting Permission: How to License and Clear Copyrighted Materials Online and Off (Book w/disk—PC)	$34.95	RIPER
How to Make Patent Drawings Yourself	$29.95	DRAW
The Inventor's Notebook	$19.95	INOT
⊡ License Your Invention (Book w/Disk—PC)	$39.95	LICE
Patent, Copyright & Trademark	$29.95	PCTM
Patent It Yourself	$46.95	PAT
Patent Searching Made Easy	$29.95	PATSE
⊙ Software Development: A Legal Guide (Book with CD-ROM)	$44.95	SFT
Trademark: Legal Care for Your Business and Product Name	$39.95	TRD
The Trademark Registration Kit (Quick & Legal Series)	$19.95	TREG

SENIORS

	PRICE	CODE
Beat the Nursing Home Trap: A Consumer's Guide to Assisted Living and Long-Term Care	$21.95	ELD
The Conservatorship Book for California	$44.95	CNSV
Social Security, Medicare & Pensions	$24.95	SOA

SOFTWARE

Call or check our website at www.nolo.com for special discounts on Software!

	PRICE	CODE
⊙ LeaseWriter CD—Windows/Macintosh	$129.95	LWD1
⊙ Living Trust Maker CD—Windows/Macintosh	$89.95	LTD3
⊙ Patent It Yourself CD—Windows	$229.95	PPC12
⊙ Personal RecordKeeper 5.0 CD—Windows/Macintosh	$59.95	RKD5
⊙ Small Business Pro 4 CD—Windows/Macintosh	$89.95	SBCD4
⊙ WillMaker 7.0 CD—Windows/Macintosh	$69.95	WMD7

Order Form

Name _____

Address _____

City _____

State, Zip _____

Daytime Phone _____

E-mail _____

Our "No-Hassle" Guarantee

Return anything you buy directly from Nolo for any reason and we'll cheerfully refund your purchase price. No ifs, ands or buts.

☐ Check here if you do not wish to receive mailings from other companies

Item Code	Quantity	Item	Unit Price	Total Price

Method of payment

☐ Check ☐ VISA ☐ MasterCard
☐ Discover Card ☐ American Express

Subtotal	
Add your local sales tax (California only)	
Shipping: RUSH $8, Basic $3.95 (See below)	
"I bought 3, Ship it to me FREE!"(Ground shipping only)	
TOTAL	

Account Number _____

Expiration Date _____

Signature _____

Shipping and Handling

Rush Delivery-Only $8

We'll ship any order to any street address in the U.S. by UPS 2nd Day Air* for only $8!

* Order by noon Pacific Time and get your order in 2 business days. Orders placed after noon Pacific Time will arrive in 3 business days. P.O. boxes and S.F. Bay Area use basic shipping. Alaska and Hawaii use 2nd Day Air or Priority Mail.

Basic Shipping—$3.95

Use for P.O. Boxes, Northern California and Ground Service.

Allow 1-2 weeks for delivery. U.S. addresses only.

For faster service, use your credit card and our toll-free numbers

Order 24 hours a day

Online	www.nolo.com
Phone	1-800-992-6656
Fax	1-800-645-0895
Mail	Nolo.com
	950 Parker St.
	Berkeley, CA 94710

Visit us online at
www.nolo.com

Take 2 minutes & Give us your 2 cents

Your comments make a big difference in the development and revision of Nolo books and software. Please take a few minutes and register your Nolo product—and your comments—with us. Not only will your input make a difference, you'll receive special offers available only to registered owners of Nolo products on our newest books and software. Register now by:

PHONE
1-800-992-6656

FAX
1-800-645-0895

EMAIL
cs@nolo.com

or **MAIL** us
this registration card

REMEMBER:
Little publishers have big ears. We really listen to you.

- - - - - - - - - - - - - - - fold here - - - - - - - - - - - - - - -

REGISTRATION CARD

NAME _____ DATE _____

ADDRESS _____

_____

CITY _____ STATE _____ ZIP _____

PHONE _____ E-MAIL _____

WHERE DID YOU HEAR ABOUT THIS PRODUCT? _____

WHERE DID YOU PURCHASE THIS PRODUCT? _____

DID YOU CONSULT A LAWYER? (PLEASE CIRCLE ONE)   YES   NO   NOT APPLICABLE _____

DID YOU FIND THIS BOOK HELPFUL?   (VERY)   5   4   3   2   1   (NOT AT ALL) _____

COMMENTS _____

_____

_____

WAS IT EASY TO USE?   (VERY EASY)   5   4   3   2   1   (VERY DIFFICULT) _____

DO YOU OWN A COMPUTER? IF SO, WHICH FORMAT? (PLEASE CIRCLE ONE)   WINDOWS   DOS   MAC

☐ If you do not wish to receive mailings from these companies, please check this box.

☐ You can quote me in future Nolo.com promotional materials. Daytime phone number _____.

BRS 1.2

nolo.com

950 Parker Street
Berkeley, CA 94710-9867

Attn: **BRS 1.2**